Babel Unhinged

Collected Essays in Philosophical
Anthropology and Cultural Criticism

Other Works by Sandy Krolick

Вероника: Сибирская Сказка (Novel)
VERONIKA: The Siberian's Tale (Novel)
The Recovery of Ecstasy: Notebooks from Siberia
Apocalypse of the Barbarians: Inquisitions on Empire
Conversations On A Country Path
Gandhi in the Postmodern Age
Recollective Resolve
Ethical Decision-making Styles
Культурныи критицизм
Myth, Mystery and Magic: Religious Imagination in Ancient Egypt
Russian Soul and Collapse of the West
Shambhala (Novel)
Misha (Novel)
On Being and Being Good
Q: Interpreting QAnon
A New Heaven and a New Earth
Philosophic Play On Culture and Society

Babel Unhinged

Collected Essays in Philosophical Anthropology and Cultural Criticism

sandy krolick, ph.d

Islands Press
New York : Altai Krai

ISBN: 978-1-7350698-6-9

Cover art courtesy of:
Sergei Prokhorov
Altai Krai, Russia

Contents

In the Folds of the Flesh

Reflections On Touch

A Tactile Ontology

Following a path charted by the late Hans Jonas, our inquiry concerning the sense of touch must proceed from two directions concurrently — from the vantage point of agency as well as that of the percipient body. In other words, we need to grasp our *haptic* sense in terms of its spontaneous movement between acting and feeling. We seek to articulate how through its very *intentionality* — extending oneself, bodying-forth, reaching out, grasping hold of something, or embracing the Other — touch is simultaneously proactive and receptive, eliciting a response from within the very folds of our flesh. As Professor Jonas confirms:

> *The living body that can die, that has a*
> *world and itself belongs to the world,*
> *that feels and itself can be felt...this*
> *body is the memento of the still unsolved*
> *question.'What is being'?* (1)

Now if Jonas is correct, then understanding the phenomenon of touch will require an ontology of the flesh, of the body — as both subject and object in a tactile world. In short, human existence must be understood in terms of embodiment first and foremost — one's capacity to touch and be touched, to feel and be felt. As Maurice Merleau-Ponty confirms: "I delve into the thickness of the world by perceptual experience."(2) Accordingly, we should now try to articulate human being from within the 'thickness' of the flesh.

And The Word Became Flesh

The primacy of touch in human relations was most recently thrown into high relief as a result of a novel coronavirus circulating among us, forcing people into on-again off-again periods of isolation and the attendant loneliness suffered in its wake. In point of fact, a person cannot long ignore the pleadings of the flesh or the deep-seated need for touch (even a handshake) in everyday life. Similarly, one cannot fail to recognize the continuous and deliberate attenuation of both in the increasingly virtual life-world that has come to characterize contemporary life. So we ask at first: Is not touch my body's original experience of itself as it palpates the world? While my eyes engage things and other persons

3

through the mediation of sight, touch presupposes the immediacy of contact — of friction, of resistance — the pressure of my body against another's physical presence in my environment.

What I discovered years ago while browsing Vladimir Dal's nineteenth century work, *An Explanatory Dictionary of the Russian Language*, confirmed what I had already learned from a decade of living on the Siberian taiga — the primacy of touch. According to Dal's lexicography, our five senses could easily be reduced to haptic perception alone: the tongue and palate, touching food; the ear, touching sound waves; the nose, touching emanations; and the eyes, rays of light. The sense of touch would appear to define the very interstices of my world through location, movement, and the reach of my flesh — both inline and outline of the 'lived-body-world' at one and the same time. Or as my late professor Paul Ricoeur might have stated, quoting his countryman Maurice Merleau-Ponty: flesh is a *"chiasm,"* the intersecting of body-as-subject and world-as-lived by the body, affording the very possibility of tactile experience — of touching and being touched. As David Katz reminds us in *The World of Touch*:

> *[T]he movement of one's own body is to*
> *touch what lighting is to vision. And like*
> *the exploratory gaze of true vision, the*
> *'knowing touch' projects us outside our*
> *body through movement. When one of*
> *my hands touches the other, the end that*
> *moves functions as subject and the other*
> *as object.* (3)

Now, if I understand correctly, in the phenomenon of touch we discover a natural intertwining of self and world, or 'Me' and 'Other.' And as the philosopher further suggests: "I cannot forget in this case that it is through my body that I go to the world."(4) Merleau-Ponty concludes:

> *Experience discloses beneath objective*
> *space, in which the body eventually*
> *finds its place, a primitive spatiality of*
> *which experience is merely the outer*
> *covering and which merges with the*
> *body's very being. To be a body is to be*
> *tied to a certain world.* (5)

In short, my body articulates itself spatially *vis-à-vis* my comportment within the world — my eyes opening into a world which touches, receives and includes them; my gaze encountering things already there, standing out within an encompassing horizon. Looking out into this horizon, something appears, a certain determinacy occurs. As my sight begins to focus, objects take on specific shape and size; they reveal a natural spatiality. But the presence of such objects within my visual field only occurs because I am not simply a gaze; I too am spatially present. "Not primarily in space, but of it," I am always, already attuned within a world through my body-as-subject. (6) As embodied, the movements and postures I assume both constitute and are constituted by the world that touches me as I reach out and touch it. There is a natural reciprocity or openness of the flesh; touching, I am also touched — both actor and recipient, subject and object of the sensation at one and the same time. Here is the real entwining of Self and Other, at the interstice of my body of flesh and the 'flesh' of the world.

Even prior to opening her eyes, a newborn feels her body through the intimacy of a mother's embrace — that is, through the sense of touch. Beginning with that first caress, the world becomes a sensual playground for her infinitely excitable flesh. For this infant, even the inanimate objects of her surroundings, what we adults might call dead matter — a stone, a tree, wind, water, fire and ice — even these are alive under her gaze, her touch; they are filled with life, passion, and being — just as they were for our primeval forebears, where vitality was everywhere, and being was the same as being alive. As Jonas reminds us:

> *[T]hough this is forgotten, the cosmos was once alive as perceived by man, and its more recent lifeless image was built up, or left over, in a continuous process of critical subtraction from its fuller original content.* (7)

What we moderns dismissively label animism or vitalism — the attributing of life and intentionality to inanimate objects or nature — was for the many millennia of pre-civilized hominid existence a simple acknowledgement of the power, the force, the capacity of nature to act; and since we are intimately part of that nature, it is a recognition of the power enabling our own movement as well. Insofar as all things share in this ability, this *pouvoir*, we are basically of the same essence, the same substance. I became acutely aware of this while resident in Siberia, living closer to the land — closer to nature and its power — understanding that we are part of the earth, the soil, as it is part of us; we share the same flesh, the same destiny!

Even my own body does not initially present me as an isolated entity, separate from the world — an ego locked up within a bag of skin. Rather, my flesh articulates my *facticity* as well as my *tactility* — a dwelling place within the powerful continuum of life. Neither am I simply a static presence within this field. I too exhibit motility and intentionality; a spontaneous capacity to move and to engage — the act of touch itself suggestive of such inherent potency, along with the dynamic configuration of space, as realized in dance, the hunt, and play, as well as in eating, sleeping, and sexual engagement.

From the simple positioning of my body, whether passively suffering or forcibly acting, my flesh exhibits a natural reflexivity, a turning back upon itself, both the breach and bridge that constitute my being-situated. This somatic facing in two directions, both inward (*proprioceptive*), and outward (*tactile*), is the ground of my own ecstatic existence; it is a pre-reflective experience of doubling, whereby I understand the potentiality of being both myself and other than myself, immersed in the power of life: my flesh, the flesh of the world!

> *Body and mind are like the inside and outside of our skin—two sides of one sleeve. And since actuality is what*

allows for empathy with others, a
civilization that loses touch with flesh
loses touch with itself. (8)

Tactility and Empathy

In our current, post-modern predicament, the question must be raised: Have we already lost touch with our senses, with ourselves? Have we lost touch with the flesh and with one another? Recall what Adam and Eve had discovered back in Big Daddy's garden of earthly delights — nakedness, intimacy, sexuality — the feeling of flesh against flesh: a primeval condition perhaps more eloquently expressed by the poet.

> *When love with one another so Inter-*
> *animates two souls … So must pure*
> *lovers' souls descend T' affections, and*
> *to faculties Which sense may reach and*
> *apprehend… (9)*

This question then — of losing touch with ourselves as well as our capacity for touch — lies at the very foundation of our current dilemma, a situation made yet more poignant by the recent inconveniences created by a novel coronavirus. But perhaps there's a remnant, a small crease in our historic march through this post-Covid world that still allows for our being-with-one-another, intimately engaged, both touching and being touched.

We should understand first and foremost that touch is not always or only about physical communion *per se*, but also about being 'in-touch-with' — a much broader medium of engagement or 'being-with' the Other. As Richard Kearney suggests: there's a genuine sense in which touch is also a 'feeling-for,' 'caring-for,' or empathically 'being-with' the Other. Of course, this may explain why our primal forebears sensed their own totemic identifications not as mere metaphors but as a means of genuine engagement-with and being-touched-by something beyond themselves, an experience of having an identity greater than oneself, attached to something more — a Platonic *metaxis* of sorts. And, perhaps touch or tactile intimacy within the most primal of human communities is not simply a matter of flesh upon flesh — although it is that as well. (10) Rather, it may be as much about the natural folding-in or conjoining of oneself symbolically with the Other as seen in relations adhering among most kinship-based societies. As Marshall Sahlins suggests:

> *In kin relationships, others become*
> *predicates of one's own existence, and*

10

vice versa... It is the integration of certain relationships, hence the participation of certain others in one's own being. As members of one another, kinsmen live each other's lives and die each other's deaths... [I]n kinship, as in relations to the cosmos in general, alterity is a condition of the possibility of being. (11)

In such settings, the very notion of the 'self' as an isolated ego — the assumption undergirding our modern conception of individuality — was either non-existent or not of primary concern among our pre-modern predecessors. In fact, for kinship-based cultures, the person was meaningfully constituted only in his or her tangible (felt) relations with other members of the tribe or clan, including a rather fluid identity shared among totem and tribe with their natural surround. Here we may note that encounters with ancestral spirits among the Amazonian Piraha — whether in dream or awake — were as real as any concrete relations between tribal members themselves. (12) In fact, within most pre-civilized cultures, a person is rarely if ever seen as a purely independent, isolated entity struggling against a foreign environment. Rather, the individual exists as an embodied instantiation of a much more

11

encompassing sense of self-in-community. Again from Sahlins we read:

> *Ethnographic reports speak of*
> *'transpersonal self' (Native Americans),*
> *of self as a 'locus of shared social*
> *relations or biographies' (Caroline*
> *Islands), of persons as 'the plural and*
> *composite site of the relationships that*
> *produced them' (New Guinea*
> *Highlands). Referring broadly to the*
> *African concept of 'the individual,'*
> *Roger Bastide writes: 'He does not exist*
> *except to the extent he is outside and*
> *different from himself.' Clearly, the self*
> *in these societies is not synonymous*
> *with the bounded, unitary and*
> *autonomous individual as we know*
> *him... Rather the individual person is*
> *the locus of multiple other selves with*
> *whom he or she is joined in mutual*
> *relations of being...* (13)

Of course, there are other examples among primitive and pre-literate cultures far too numerous to recount where departed kinsmen, helper spirits, or other phantom guides engage auditorily, visually, and even tactilely with those still among the living

— with countrymen, friends, family, shamans, priests, or visionaries. In short, embodiment in one form or another — being touched, in-touch, or even touching the hand of God — remains central to our human tragedy. And, remember that even the risen Jesus of Nazareth appeared to his disciples in the flesh.

The Frailty of Flesh

There's an important distinction still to be drawn between simple tactile sensations and the feel of flesh upon flesh. The impressions I receive when I reach out and touch something are not quite the same as what I experience when I feel or embrace another person. And this is the real mystery of flesh, where a "mere touch-impression" is transformed from a simple "tactile encounter" into an act of "feeling another body."(14)

Touching the Other elicits a singular sensation originating in the natural reflexivity of the act itself. Touching another individual, I am acutely aware of how he or she feels when being touched by me. This experiencing of one's own flesh in and through touching or being touched by another is at the heart of our experience of sexual intimacy. In no other tactile encounter is the flesh so utterly absorbed —

and two souls so completely inter-animated — as in the ecstatic feeling that occurs in the mutuality of carnal relations. Here the intimacy of touch viscerally reveals the transcendent possibilities of embodiment — the potential for being myself and being other than or greater than myself. Again, I recall the words of the poet:

> *Our bodies why do we forbear?... We*
> *owe them thanks, because they thus Did*
> *us, to us, at first convey, Yielded their*
> *senses' force to us, Nor are dross to us,*
> *but allay. On man, heaven's influence*
> *works not so, But that it first imprints*
> *the air; So soul into the soul may flow,*
> *Though it to body first repair.* (15)

The feel of my lover's body, the pressure of flesh against flesh, generates heat, stimulating as well our sense of smell and taste, while the tongue, in licking — like the hand, in touching — body's-forth this same cutaneous experience, making direct appeal to *appetence* and pressing fulfillment. The eyes are perhaps the least engaged in this intimate play of the flesh, with almost all awareness gathered around touch, smell and taste, and to some degree hearing — listening to one another's sounds, breathings, and silences.

What is it about touch, and in particular the feel of another's flesh that we find so welcoming and yet, at times, so fearsome? Of course, there is a deeply emotional satisfaction in human touch: the hearty handshake, an extended arm to hold, a shoulder to cry on, an affectionate hug, a gentle caress, a loving embrace, or a warm body to envelop me. But there is another, darker side as well: the battering, assault, beating, trauma, and the attendant suffering of pain.

The more I reflect on our current historical circumstance, the clearer it seems that the world today is in desperate need of pleasurable touch. Of course, human life is and remains a mediated existence — sensual fulfillment always something outstanding, still to be realized anew. But, it is this very mediation between self and world, or self and Other, that gives rise to appetition in the first place. As Hans Jonas summarizes: like all animal existence, human being is and remains essentially passionate. (16)

Throughout my youth and early adulthood, I had never seriously considered the degree to which the touch of the flesh was such an elemental need. But once discovered, never would that recognition be forgotten. And, as I later came to see, the primacy of our haptic sense — of touching and being touched

— provided the somatic basis for a more organic mode of recollection. In short, there seemed to be some primal, if not instinctual, memory-trace associated with tactile sensation itself — a muted, natural recollection buried deep within the folds of my flesh. In their own work, *Sex At Dawn*, Christopher Ryan and Cacilda Jetha are clear about this hardwired need — not simply for physical connection, but for intimacy as well.

> *Homo sapiens evolved to be*
> *shamelessly, undeniably, inescapably*
> *sexual... But these preconscious*
> *impulses remain our biological*
> *baseline, our reference point, the zero in*
> *our own personal number system.* (17)

On the other hand, physical isolation, if even for only brief periods, can prove psychologically unsettling — a result of internality, of being cut off from normal human interaction — unable to reach out and touch one another in friendship, intimacy, or even conflict. Our body of flesh is not so much an accoutrement, additive to our human nature; it is part and parcel of who we are, as well as how we see and position ourselves *vis-à-vis* the Other. Yet, in an increasingly digitized, virtual life-world, further accentuated by the likes of a novel virus,

16

many of us have literally been left desperate for even the most casual experience of human touch. And there is a kind of melancholy tied directly to this inability to reach out and touch one another, to bind ourselves through being together in the flesh.

Today, separated from countless strangers by only thin walls, tiny earbuds and hectic schedules, we assume a desolate sense of isolation must have weighed heavily on our ancestors, wandering over their windswept prehistoric landscapes. But in fact, this seemingly common-sense assumption couldn't be more mistaken. The social lives of foragers were characterized by a depth and intensity of community few of us could imagine (or perhaps tolerate).

> *From the first morning of birth to the final mourning of death, a forager's life was one of intense, constant interaction, interrelation, and interdependence.* (18)

'Touched by' and 'Cared for'

It would seem in conclusion that we are by nature intertwined, inter-involved and, to that extent, responsible for one another; indeed, this all-too-

17

human burden is reflected in the very structure of our being. As the philosopher says, we are fundamentally 'being-there' *alongside* and *with* other people, even when we are ostensibly alone. This existential structure of 'being-with' implicates us in a profound circle of reciprocity whereby **care** for the Other — including the sharing of vital resources — seems only natural. (19) It is simply the human thing to do, rooted in the genetic makeup of our species, our Pleistocene heritage. Martin Heidegger designates this the essential "Care-structure" (*Sorge*) of human existence. It is also significant to note that etymologically 'care' derives from Old English (*caru*) as well as Old Saxon and Gothic (*kara*) — referring to one's 'concern' or even 'anxious apprehension' attendant upon recognition of one's finite nature. In any event, Heidegger reminds us of its import with a short fable recorded by Franz Bücheler — a myth concerning the nature of Care — linked as it is to our concrete relations, including our fundamental vulnerability.

> *Once when 'Care' was crossing a river,*
> *she saw some clay; she thoughtfully*
> *took a piece and began to shape it.*
> *While she was thinking about what she*
> *had made, Jupiter came by. 'Care'*

asked him to give it spirit, and this he
gladly granted. But when she wanted
her name to be bestowed upon it,
Jupiter forbade this and demanded that
it be given his name instead. While
'Care' and Jupiter were arguing, Earth
arose, and desired that her name be
conferred upon the creature, since she
had offered it part of her body. They
asked Saturn to be the judge. And
Saturn gave them the following
decision, which seemed to be just:
"Since you, Jupiter, have given its spirit,
you should receive that spirit at death;
and since you, Earth, have given its
body, you shall receive its body. But
since 'Care' first shaped this creature,
she shall possess it as long as it lives.
And because there is a dispute among
you as to its name, let it be called
'homo,' for it is made out of humus
(earth)." (20)

Here we come full circle, acknowledging the
tentative and precarious nature of life in the body,
accepting the reality of death cradled within our
own flesh, at the same time recognizing the world-
openness which this concrete body of flesh affords

us, including our capacity to touch and be touched by the Other. Herein lies the foundation of our quest for genuine human contact — not only for physical touch and the intimacy afforded by the flesh, but for caring and being cared-for by one another. As Professor Jonas concludes:

> *That life is mortal is indeed its*
> *fundamental contradiction, but this also*
> *belongs inseparably to its essence. Life*
> *cannot at any time be imagined apart*
> *from its mortality... [we are] free, but*
> *dependent; isolated but in necessary*
> *contact; seeking contact, but*
> *destructible because of it: conversely,*
> *no less threatened by want of contact:*
> *endangered thus on both sides, by both*
> *the tremendous power and brittleness of*
> *the world, and standing on the narrow*
> *ridge between.* (21)

Positioned on a kind of precipice — open to the Other, but distracted by our own frailty — we venture out hand-in-hand, bodying-forth our fears as well as our desires, displaying our concern as well as our profoundly human capacity to care-for and be cared-for.

In the folds of our flesh, where the most visceral and engaging emotions of human existence lie, the very concreteness of life in the body is reflected by our various moods as well as our approach to the Other: anxiety, worry, apprehension, concern and care. Recognition of our own finitude, our own potentiality for not-being, is what provides the impetus, the desire, to seek out and embrace the Other — to commune, conjoin, and enjoy the camaraderie as well as the intimacy of being together in the flesh. We long for the Other, for connection, for mutual support — to touch and be touched — physically as well as emotionally, psychologically. These are the hallmarks of human life in the body in the world.

Notes

1. Hans Jonas, *The Phenomenon of Life: Toward a Philosophical Biology,* p. 19

2. Maurice Merleau-Ponty, *Phenomenology of Perception*, p. 204

3. See, Ibid, p. 315

4. Ibid, p. 316

5. Ibid, p. 148

6. Ibid

7. Hans Jonas, *The Phenomenon of Life*, p. 12

8. Richard Kearney, *Touch: Recovering Our Most Vital Sense*, p. 47

9. John Donne, *The Ecstasy*

10. See, for example, the study by Chris Ryan and Cacilda Jetha, *Sex At Dawn*

11. Marshall Sahlins, *The Western Illusion of Human Nature,* pp. 46-48

12. Daniel L. Everett, *Don't Sleep There are Snakes*, p. 137

13. Marshall Sahlins, pp. 46-48

14. Hans Jonas, *The Phenomenon of Life*, p. 141

15. John Donne, *The Ecstasy*

16. Hans Jonas, *The Phenomenon of Life*, pp. 106

17. Christopher Ryan and Cacilda Jetha, *Sex at Dawn*, p. 46

18. Ibid, p. 88

19. Morton Fried, *The Evolution of Political Society: An Essay in Political Anthropology*

20. Martin Heidegger, *Being and Time*, p. 25

21. Hans Jonas, *Memoirs*, p. 230

The Eyes Have It
An Essay In Philosophical Anthropology

The wood nymphs vanished as the woods
filled with trailer camps. Water sprites have
been crowded out by submarines and scuba
divers. (1)

In view of all the time we devote to pouring over
internet screens, our eyes firmly cemented to
graphic digital displays in an increasingly visual
world, the following questions beg for answers.
Why did our sense of sight eventually come to
dominate perceptual experience, subordinating the
remaining richness of our complex and multifaceted
sensorium? Alternatively, to what extent did this
reorganization of our Pleistocene-honed senses lead
to the loss of a more primal participation in the
'earthly sensuous'? What may have led to such
reorganization and under what organizing principle?
In short, what has intervened to come between the
animating forces of our primal hominid perceptions
and the fullness of that plenum just beyond the
reach of our touch?

The answers may be complicated, if not troubling. Among the issues we need consider are the following shifts in social organization and culture: the movement away from nomadic foraging to the beginnings of agriculture; from a primal engagement with natural periodicities to a strictly unidirectional sense of clock time; from oral traditions to a literate culture; from complex 'polysemic' totemic identifications to a strictly univocal law of identity; from a tactile experience of the earthly sensuous to the ascendancy of vision in a newly structured perceptual hierarchy. Referring to this generally as a "diminishment of the world-as-presence," Walter Ong reminds us that insofar as experience is grounded in the senses, it appears to be grounded in all simultaneously. We speak of a 'sense' of presence, rather than a sight, sound, smell, taste, or touch of presence. (2)

But, what really happened to force the truncation of our primal sense of presence? As renowned paleo-anthropologist, Richard Leaky, notes:

> *Every biologist knows that when a basic change occurs in a species' pattern of subsistence, other changes usually follow.* (3)

To understand the causes behind these bio-socio-cultural changes in our species' development, we must begin by taking Leaky's claim seriously. A shift in our predecessors 'patterns of subsistence' or food acquisition techniques from foraging to agriculture, and from nomadic to domestic life-ways, must have involved a substantive change in early modern humans' (*Homo sapiens*) mental and visual senses. In other words, this transformation must have had a direct and distinctive impact on how these earliest humans saw and experienced the world — their view of the visual surround — including their relationships within the natural environment. Humanity began to see with new eyes, and apparently, the encompassing surround of nature was increasingly seen as an independent field just waiting to be mastered with the dawn of the new and powerful process of instrumental reason.

Wandering, hunting, and gathering food in the wild, once indicative of our primal forebears' familiarity with the territory, was slowly eclipsed, only to be replaced by stationary observation posts where sedentary overseers stood watch over newly planted fields of grain spread out before hopeful eyes just awaiting the cornucopia. Not to be lost sight of here were the numerous visual metaphors that became ever more critical to a domesticated lifestyle, while other senses seemed to atrophy, fading into the background as so much noise.

Clearly, there was a revision underway in the perceptual hierarchy of our forebears that emerged in association with the transition in food acquisition and production technologies. This new hierarchy was defined by more domesticated sensibilities, watched over by an emerging focus on the planning and planting of crops. The visual field itself now appeared like a flat-screen projection of things 'out there' revealing itself as ever more pedestrian and slowly but surely becoming emptied of vitality as the eclipsing of our sensory apparatus continued unabated. (4) Don't misunderstand me; vision is indeed a noble and wonderful endowment without which our survival as a species would be unimaginable. But, as Hans Jonas still warns us:

> *Vision is only the part-function of a whole body, which experiences its dynamic involvement with the environment in the feeling of its position and changes of position. The 'possession' of a body of which the eyes are a part is indeed the primal fact of our 'spatiality'. Without this background of non-*

visual, corporeal feeling and the accumulated
experience of performed motion, the eyes
alone would not supply knowledge of space.
(5)

We may easily forget that our own sense of space
emerges as we feel our bodies move within a world
that reaches out and receives our flesh — that
motility and gesture betrays the body as a point of
departure on the world, an openness to its presence,
an intertwining between our senses and the earthly
sensuous that reciprocates and corresponds to our
every move. It is only the assumption of a purely
interior self (an internalized ego), hypothesized by a
rationalist metaphysics, and granting privileged
position to sight alone, that creates the impression
of a purely objective world in the first place. But
this reductive impression does not correspond to
what our bodies tell us every day, even before we
open our eyes, extending our feet blindly, only to be
met by the ground beneath us. As David Abrams
teases,

Prior to all our verbal reflections, at the level
of our spontaneous sensorial engagement with
the world around us, we are all animists. (6)

So why is it that sight alone has achieved such a lofty, even commanding, status among the senses? Why is the subjectivity of the body itself shunned, while vision takes on an independent but truncated life of its own? For whatever reason, we find that in Greek thought, sight had already been elevated — "hailed as the most excellent of the senses." In fact, visual metaphors constantly emerge to describe this as the highest activity of mind — *theoria*. From Plato onward, all of Western philosophy honors sight above all else, referring to it alternatively as the "eye of the soul" and "the light of reason." Aristotle confirms this in the opening remarks of his *Treatise on Metaphysics*:

> *ALL men by nature desire to know. An indication of this is the delight we take in our senses; for even apart from their usefulness they are loved for themselves; and above all others the sense of sight.* (7)

Despite Aristotle's rather enthusiastic endorsement of sight, we should repeat that the very motility of the body — its ability to move, to act, to reach out and touch — is always, already a "factor in the very constitution of seeing and the seen world

29

themselves, much as this genesis is forgotten in the conscious result."(8) So we again come back to the intentionality of lived-body itself.

Discussing the social development of toddlers among New Guinea forest-dwelling hunter-gatherer-gardeners living on the southern slopes of the Kratke Range just after Western contact in the early 1960s, Richard Sorenson wrote:

> *When babies began acquiring verbal speech, their words and sentences floated out atop a sophisticated body-language already well in place. Even after acquiring spoken language, tactile-talk continued taking precedence in much of daily life. It conveyed affect better. It was faster and more direct. Most of all it touched more deeply and more quickly into the hearts and minds of others. Tactile-talk was affect-talk. It integrated the spontaneous affect of individuals, often many at a time. So adept did young children become at this that they would at times merge actions into wordless synchrony.* (9)

So what turned our Pleistocene 'sense of presence' into a Holocene-born enemy of original participation in the earthly sensuous? In other words, what forced our visual sense into objectifying the world as something 'out-there' and wholly distinct from us, a spectacle to be observed, resources to be depleted, or objects to be manipulated — where even other people become simple 'marks' or 'targets' in our sights? When and how did vision become an alienating sense? It is likely that such transformation proceeded in conjunction with other key cultural developments, literacy, for example — with the externalization and objectification of speech in the written word. As Walter Ong has suggested,

> *The world of a dominantly oral or aural culture is dynamic and relatively unpredictable, an event-world rather than an object-world... Sound signals the present use of power, since sound must be in active production in order to exist at all.* (10)

There was both power and polysemy in the verbal utterance, a special power not felt in the written word. But the visual/linear nature of reading and writing, as opposed to the oral/aural surround of speech, contributed to elevating this new use of vision, leading ineluctably to the recognition of a new logistic. Now there was a rationale for structuring the written word, allowing for the 'lawful' codification of an increasingly objectified world, the 'discovery' of material causality, and a growing commitment to unidirectional time.

As Tim Ingold has argued:

> *The responsibility for reducing the world to a realm of manipulable objects lies not with the hegemony of vision but with a 'certain narrow conception of thought.' And it is this conception, too, that has led to the reduction of vision — that is, to its construal as a sensory modality specialized in the appropriation and manipulation of an objectified world.* (11)

Of course, this may have been forced by the break-up of pre-urban clans, the growth of urban life, and the accumulation of newly estranged peoples within the anonymity of a city center. These conditions demanded a profound change in the nature of

human communication, including the removal of
any of the ambiguity in primal speech, together with
the articulation of a strictly univocal semantic. Such
linguistic conceptualization was only effected with
the invention of the syllogism, early on perfected by
the Greeks, and applied by legislators, scientists,
and other specialists down through the ages. With
this newly established logistic, universal statements
were related to particular circumstances, leading to
logical legal and scientific conclusions.

> *This [tripartite logistic] form becomes a*
> *foundation layer of both the internal and*
> *external life of the West. We can call [this]*
> *logistic stratum of the univocal linguistic*
> *hierarchy the curriculum of the West.*(12)

This is how natural laws were 'discovered' and
social laws born. It was by means of the syllogism
— the core of Western logic — that cause and effect
would now be properly related on the horizontal
axis of a unidirectional timeline, past actions
identified as the causal basis of present or future
effects.

And so, it would be under that ever-watchful eye of
Father Time — occupying his sacred place in the

clock tower at the center of the town square — that the rational business of civilization was to be carried out: marking time, managing resources, assigning liability, measuring risk, buying and selling commodities in the open marketplace — with the smell of the animate world now receding further from view. The institutionalization of civic life, now regulated by the clock and managed with social and economic laws, would further solidify a growing sense of isolation, competitiveness, and the emergence of purely self-regarding behavior that would forever haunt modern societies.

I wager that it was in the full ascendancy of sight with Aristotle, and establishment of a hyper-visualism born of this new logistic, that the experience of primal participation was finally lost, buried beneath accreted layers constituting this new 'curriculum of the West.' And while original participation was never fully extinguished, it became muted along with the richness of the earthly sensuous upon which it fed.

Maybe now we can better appreciate the ineluctable pull of the ubiquitous and brightly glowing computer screen and its representations of a remote world out-there, a fully externalized, albeit virtual reality, where we can enter into disembodied relationships, engage in private war games, or deliver live drone attacks on foreign soils without ever once moving our bodies, touching the ground, getting our hands dirty, or otherwise sensing the taste of blood on our tongues, the smell of earth in our nostrils, hearing the cries of the dying, or feeling the brush of naked flesh against flesh.

Notes:

(1) Walter Ong, "World as View and Event," *American Anthropologist*, 71, 1969, p. 647

(2) Ibid, 1969, p. 646

(3) Leaky, Richard, *The Origin of Humankind*, Basic Books, 1994, p. 55

(4) Jonathan Z. Smith, 'The Map is not the Territory'

(5) Jonas, Hans, *The Phenomenon of Life*, Northwestern University Press, 2001, p.154

(6) Abrams, David, *The Spell of the Sensuous,* Vintage, 1996, p. 57

(7) Aristotle, *Treatise on Metaphysics*, Book 1

(8) Jonas, Op. Cit., p.152

(9) Sorenson, Richard, "Anthropology as an epistemological problem," *Tribal Epistemologies: Essays in the Philosophy of Anthropology*, The Anthropik Network, 1997

(10) Ong, Walter, "World as View and Event," *American Anthropologist*, 1969, p. 71

(11) Ingold, Tim, *The Perception of the Environment*, Routledge, 2011, p. 287

(12) Bram, Marvin, *Recovery Of The West:An Essay In Symbolic History*, Xlibris, 2002, p. 26

Babel Unhinged

*As the written word began speaking, the
stones fell silent... the trees became mute,
and other animals dumb.* (1)

There is general consensus that history began at Ur,
a city-state in Sumer, near the Persian Gulf in the
area of ancient Mesopotamia. It was there that the
first kings issued — and had transcribed into written
code — the first civil laws approximately five-
thousand years ago. With this development, literacy
quickly replaced oral tradition, while the written
word became imbued with magical powers formerly
attributed to the spoken word itself.

Coincident with this new technology of writing,
there emerged entirely novel ways of thinking,
acting, and interacting within the world. In fact,
with those first inscribed laws, citizenship was born.
Overwhelming evidence from the history of
religion, anthropology, archeology, paleontology,
and ethnography strongly reinforces the view that a
qualitatively different set of perceptions emerged
with this transition to literacy. Human community
itself was transformed from small egalitarian,

kinship based bands of nomadic hunter-gatherers, into more sedentary, hierarchically structured groups based primarily on plant and animal domestication. This transition erupted dramatically onto the scene near the close of the Neolithic Era.

These cognitive changes produced resounding reverberations for all generations that would follow, entrenched as humanity would become in new organizational hierarchies — the formal institutions of civil society. It was literacy, giving special prominence to the written word, that would provide the momentum in developing political institutions, world religions, and the burgeoning sciences. Borrowing terminology, I will call this new logistic model according to which reality was thereafter constituted, the curriculum of the West. An incipient temperament for this emergent worldview affected every dimension of life as civilization spread and cities continued to populate the globe over subsequent millennia.

It is interesting, in this regard, to note how the newly domesticated and orderly rows of plowed fields — those 'amber waves of grain' — led to urban surpluses. These surpluses were, in turn, stored and accounted for through columns of numbers on linear tablets (inscribed records) of the earliest kingdoms and nation states. The haphazard plots of pre-urban horticulturalists were simply not comparable with the tilled and plowed fields of the agriculturalist, just as the meandering herds of sheep among the earliest shepherds cannot compare to the meticulously aligned metal stalls of the modern abattoir. And the language of control, the written document, was key to building the associated hierarchies that would henceforth manage the herds, the fields, the supplies, and the citizens, as well as the outsiders. Here we find not only the first signs of writing, but documented codes of social control as well. Legal institutions, advocates and judges, guilt and innocence, along with police forces and the military were born in that self-same moment of our earliest history. It is here that the trajectory of Western Civilization was set.

This view of the world established and entrenched itself, memorializing our changed relationship with nature. The environment, the world as given, was thereafter emptied of intrinsic significance aside from that which these new humans and the logic of the written word attributed to it. This linguistic turn, by objectifying life, destroyed the power and thickness of the given world, leading ineluctably to the de-animation of nature and subsequent elaboration of mythological religious powers — gods, goddesses, or other supernatural entities. All the major world religions have this transcendent construction at their core, whether we call it Allah, Brahman, God, or Yahweh. Even those polytheists, the ancient Romans and Greeks, fell victim to the same illusion, the only difference being that they had numerous deities, as did the Hindus before them. The philosophers for their part also sought out true reality beyond the phenomenal world in a hypothetical 'noumenal' realm. Once again, this reinforced the fundamental assumption about some immutable 'Being' that gives life or meaning to the world of "becoming." And, it was this *diremption* — the forceful and artificial bifurcation of being and becoming, of sacred and profane — that is its legacy today.

Like its first cousin, the human sciences (and its bastard brother, the natural sciences), historical religions have lived off this fundamental dualism haunting human conception since the birth of history. Preliterate humanity on the other hand seemingly made no such distinctions, experiencing the world as a living, breathing being. There was a felt power and motility shared with all sentient beings, even with what we would call inanimate nature. It is for this reason that pre-literate consciousness has been called 'participatory'. Tribal members fused with their totem animal, intertwined with their environments. Indeed, from their perspective there was no substantive difference between themselves and the totem; they were essentially of one substance or consubstantial. We must not be confused here. It is not as if they thought like us, only with incorrect judgments; they did not think the way we do at all. It was qualitatively a different mode of perceiving and experiencing the world altogether. They did not see from a detached or objective perspective; indeed, we cannot say that they saw any "things" at all in the sense that we speak of things today in space-time. Rather they participated things, experiencing their world differently from how we configure our world today.

Let us take, for example, some words from the *Book of Genesis*, the story concerning the Tower of Babel. This biblical tale is not necessarily concerned with the multiplicity of tongues. It is rather about the overarching integrity of a universal logic that has taken hold of civic life; specifically, it is about the written word's unique ability to subordinate and unify a disparate citizenry within a shared grammar and worldview. I would say the tale of Babel represents a mythic recognition of the trajectory of the written word — literacy's capacity for disambiguation and hierarchization, enabling greater degrees of command and control. The story most probably expressed a muted regrets over the loss of polysemy, along with the freedom and intimacy that preceded the birth of cities, kingship, and written codes of conduct. Why else would the story speak so directly about divine intervention confusing the tongues of man?

> *But the Lord came down to see the city*
> *and the tower which the sons of men*
> *had built. And the Lord said, Indeed the*
> *people are one and they all have one*
> *language, and this is what they begin to*
> *do; now nothing that they propose will*
> *be withheld from them.* (2)

The building of cities, the concrete establishment of civilization — the Tower of Babel — were all dependent upon the precision of the written word and the hierarchical control it afforded the literati in the imperial court. No doubt, much was gained with the leap into literacy — the recording of events, the significance of the recent past and the potential value of the future. As well, literacy provided the linchpin for establishing bureaucratic structure and law. This, in turn, enabled management of the great menagerie of the human community along with the other possibilities civil society now afforded. Yet, in this moment there was also born silent regret for a recent past perhaps poorly lived as well as anxiety over a future that was as of yet uncertain. In short, there now was the weighty terror of historical consciousness and the personal realization that someday 'I too shall die'.

No doubt that these developments — agriculture, urbanization, and literacy — had an incalculable impact on human perception and consciousness over the ensuing millennia, producing entirely novel ways of constituting and controlling the external world. Reflectively detaching itself from a living environment, consciousness now constituted reality differently after the birth of cities than it had previously, when humans still were intimately woven into the fabric of the natural environment perceptually and mythologically. This cognitive change produced resounding reverberations for all generations to follow, entrenched, as humanity would become in new organizational hierarchies that would appear — the formal institutions of civil society. Giving special prominence to this organizing logistic, literacy provided momentum to both the political and scientific objectification of nature and, consequently, to human relations.

An incipient temperament for this burgeoning logistic, together with a newly constructed worldview, affected every dimension of life as civilization spread and cities continued to populate the globe over the subsequent millennia. Again, it was our linguistic turn — destroying the power and thickness of the given surround — that led to a de-animation of the natural world and subsequent construction of transcendent powers before which we still bow today — gods and goddesses, the 'noumena,' or finally, the abstract laws of modern physics.

Notes:

(1) David Abram, *The Spell of the Sensuous*, p. 131

(2) *Genesis*, 11:5-9

LOST IN TRANSLATION

Altai State Pedagogical University, Barnaul, Russia, 2018

> *"Because such fingers need to knit*
> *That subtle knot which makes us men*
> *So must pure lovers souls descend*
> *To affection and to faculties*
> *That sense may reach and apprehend*
> *To our bodies turn we then."*
> (Jon Donne, *The Ecstasy*)

> *"The spoken word is a gesture,*
> *and its meaning, a world."*
> (Maurice Merleau-Ponty,
> *Phenomenology of Perception*)

My eyes open onto a world that touches, receives, and includes them. Looking into the horizon, things appear before me and around me. My gaze rests upon objects already present, standing-out within my visual surround. As my sight focuses, things assume specific shapes and sizes; they reveal a spatial presence. But the existence of such 'objects' within my field of vision only occurs because I am not simply a gaze. I too have a spatial presence and

45

posture. I am always, already present in the world ~ my body itself, not only an object among others, but a perceiving subject as well. It is with respect to this primal sense of being-present, that is to say, it is in relation to my body-as-subject, that things can appear at all, disclosing themselves as coexisting with me.

I am an embodied-subject in the world, and the movements and postures that I assume both constitute and are constituted by a world in which I find myself always, already thrown. Physically engaged in this world, my movements and gestures, and even my sight, reaches out towards other objects, other presences — thereby qualifying spatial relationships, and ultimately providing me a sense of order and orientation. In fact, shapes, locations, movements, and events all have significance for me, only because I am already projected into the world through the very flesh, muscles, and 'motor intentionality' of my body.

Meaning emerges, first and foremost, on the ground of this primal intentionality of my flesh. So what has all this to do with language, linguistics, or the problem of translation and pedagogy? Basically, it has to do with the relation of language and linguistics to key issues in the human sciences, and how those issues circle-back around to the challenges of translation and the underlying problem of human understanding articulated by Wilhelm Dilthey in 19th and early 20th Century Germany.

Living in Altai Krai without a full-throated capacity to speak, nor a readily available comprehension of, spoken Russian, I have had to watch, engage, and learn to grasp conversational meaning through physical gesture, bodily posture, movement, social context, vocal tone, and facial expression. It has been, if you will, an existential requirement for me. Of necessity then, I have become somewhat adept at reading the unspoken tone and texture of voice, facial expression, and even the silence that often hovers obliquely between people. This has been an education in 'cross-cultural' communication which, I suggest, underlies all human understanding, and therefore must ground all acts of translation.

I want to suggest that speech, as it relates to linguistic meaning, parallels physical gesture in its own relation to the body's unique motor-intentionality. In speech, as in bodily gesture, the individual is concerned not so much with the process of signification but rather, with what is meant, pointed to, or intended in the signifying act. I would further suggest that every word, every speech-act, already rests upon a pre-verbal bodily posture ~ a gestural sense whereby the world is originally taken-up meaningfully in lived-experience. Language, in its first and most basic movement — as speech — thus makes explicit what was already implicit within the gestures of the body-as-subject.

Now, if we look back into the obscure and shadowy origins of language, we find that before the written word there was only speech ~ primeval oral traditions passed down by word of mouth from generation to generation, elder to younger. The earliest known writing system, Cuneiform, invented by the Sumerians, only emerged about six thousand years ago in Mesopotamia (the Ancient Near East), coincident with the birth of cities and the establishment of empires -- in short, with the rise of civilization and history. We began making history only when we began to write history!

This was humankind's momentous invention, necessitated in large measure by the shift from nomadic to domesticated lifeways. On the heels of agriculture and the birth of cities, it became necessary to develop uniform codes of economic, social, and political control. Only in this way could king and kingdom handle the gathering together of diverse and unrelated village, clan or tribal members, now as urban strangers — within and beyond the city walls. This development demanded a severe change in the nature of human interaction and communication, including the removal of any ambiguity or polysemy inherent in primal speech. Even the earliest instances of urban life necessitated the articulation of a strictly univocal, disambiguated, written code.

However, modern formal linguistic rationalization finally emerged with the invention of the syllogism, early perfected by the Greeks several thousand years later, and recast by scientists, legislators, and politicians down through the ages. According to syllogistic reasoning, universal statements are related to particular circumstances within a specific logistic framework, leading to clear and unambiguous legal or scientific conclusions. It all comes down to "precise words and correct syntax... that is where social laws are made and natural laws are made or discovered" (Bram, *The Recovery of the West*). But, we must never forget that underling the various strata of codified rules ~ syntactic, semantic or logistic ~ that constitute modern linguistic theory, there remains a pre-linguistic (unspoken but not silent) field of bodily (motor) intentionality (i.e., 'meaning') giving birth to the very possibility of a world full of language.

I would further suggest that language, and in its first instance, as speech, bestows meaning in much the same way that a physical gesture imparts meaning, embodying its sense within the act itself. Speaking is itself a gesture, an act of human embodiment. Speech-acts are themselves concrete (oral-aural), positional (disclosing a specific location or perspective), and directed (intending something). The initial movement from silence to speech is thus NOT a movement from non-meaning to meaning. Rather it is a "movement from the implicit to the explicit, from ambiguity already pregnant with signification to the expressed significance of speech. If meaning is 'born' it is because [bodily gesture] is already pregnant with that very possibility." (Don Ihde, "Singing the World: Language and Perception," N. Gillan, ed., *The Horizons of the Flesh*, SIU, 1973, 71)

With respect to its concreteness, we always, already know that the spoken word is intimately connected with presence. The very evanescence of speech gives the speech-act a privileged relationship to the present. As sound, speech "must emanate from a source here and now discernibly active, with the result that involvement with [speech] is involvement with here-and-now existence and activity." (Walter Ong, *The Presence of the Word*, 1981: 111-112) When we hear a sound in the night we know something is out there; and when we hear words being spoken, we know someone is speaking. A palpable and identifiable action is occurring in and through the event of speech; and we call this communication. But lest we forget, it is the body's own 'motor intentionality' that allows this very possibility. The body itself communicates, even before speech, with gesture, and even in silence ~ e.g., in pose, posture, and muscular tension. This is the proto-linguistic foundation of all linguistic meaning.

In brief, I am offering the following metaphor for consideration: prior to and underlying the formal linguistic structures of any language, there exist pre-linguistic relations embedded in the very folds of our flesh. This pre-linguistic signifying power provides both structural support and foundational impetus to a culture's concrete speech-acts. The cultural specificity of such pre- or proto-linguistic gestural acts (let's call them a dance) also suggests that authentic translation across disparate linguistic (and cultural) communities must always suffer as a result, always losing something of its existential veracity and signifying power. Why? It is because of the silence that both grounds and surrounds this motor intentionality of embodied subjectivity along with the unspoken cultural suppositions or pre-dispositions out of which each speech-act grows.

Given the centrality of the body and of the community which is its immediate horizon (the body politic), the problem for translators is the culturally specific experience of embodiment that lies at the root of each unique tradition, including the physical and tonal cues, as well as the silences that serve, sometimes unwittingly, to unmask the intent (or meaning) in any given linguistic event. These are untranslatable elements embodied and embedded within a cultural style and its language. There is literally a 'body' of meanings underlying the linguistic strata and deep structures of any given language. And it is this body of meanings hidden in

the very folds of the flesh, that most often are non-transferable into another
tongue.

There is something essential that always gets lost in translation. And, as Bill Murray, "Sometimes you have to go halfway around the world to come full circle." This is what I have come to understand. I do not question the value of textual translation, nor the obvious need for translation pedagogy. These are real necessities in our highly globalized, and increasingly interconnected planet. Yet, ours is a world where cultural difference and distinctiveness is being erased by the march of a curriculum unleashed with the ancient Sumerians and refined by the Greeks many thousands of years ago. It was upon this foundational logistic that scientific and technological progress established themselves, laying the basis for all advances, including modern systems of communication, systems that not only connect us, but increasingly tend to control us, often times unwittingly. It is our job as educators to insure that students understand not simply how to translate, but recognize as well what is hidden and at risk of being lost in translation ~ differences that emerge from the very flesh and bones and the soul of a people.

On Being and Being Good

Bergen County Ethical Culture Society, New Jersey, July, 2020

> *For those who are awake*
> *there is one common world,*
> *while those who sleep*
> *each turn away into their own,*
> (Heraclitus of Ephesus, *Fragment 89*)

Notwithstanding the fact that the first codes of conduct were etched on clay tablets in the earliest city-states of the ancient Near East more than four millennia ago (1), ethical norms have long been construed as issuing from, and largely dependent upon, diverse spiritual or sacred traditions, much like those divine commandments handed down by Moses at Mount Sinai to the Israelites as a guide to living the 'good life' — a life lived in accordance with Yahweh's law. Certainly, such religiously grounded prescriptions have served, more or less admirably, for a good portion of humanity over the centuries. And they've done so largely on faith. For others, the atheists or religiously unaffiliated among us, such norms seem to have a more modest origin, emerging from the disparate secular and humanly crafted codicils of a civil society or collective.

Yet, despite the surplus of directives enjoining our allegiance or compliance, a basic question cries out to be answered: What do we mean when we recognize someone as a 'good' or 'moral' person? Regardless of those prescriptions issuing from diverse historical traditions, is there a universally applicable and identifiable kernel — not just within communities of the faithful, but relative to our common humanity — that may be recognized as anchoring ethical behavior? Or are all such directives merely relative to specific revelations or the vicissitudes of historical circumstance, and imposed upon the unwashed masses as a civic requirement? How do we approach this question of an ethical footing valid everywhere and always? Is there anything within the structure of our experience — an ontological bearing if you will — that we would readily recognize as the organic basis of a moral sensibility? In this regard, I'm guided by Hans Jonas's contention that there is "an ontological basis for ethics," in other words, that being implies obligation. Or, as he states in his *Memoirs*,

...being can tell us something about
how we should live, but above all about
the responsibilities that we human
beings, acting consciously and freely,
must fulfill. (2)

This, then, is our underlying concern: the ethical implications of being, or alternatively, what 'being' has to do with 'being good.'

I.

Along the fertile crescent in the ancient Near-East thousands of mist-laden years before the birth of philosophy, the world was engulfed in "a peculiar type of concrete thought" — that which today we call 'myth'. Our earliest progenitors lived in a world where the hard and fast distinctions we draw among things today were not so clearly delineated — where mystery and magic enlivened a more storied kind of reflection. It was a world appearing to our earliest ancestors as "neither inanimate nor empty but redundant with life... where every phenomenon confronting man — the thunderclap, the sudden shadow, the eerie and unknown clearing in the woods, the stone which suddenly hurts him when he stumbles while hunting" (3) — where anything and everything could and did appear as a vital force to be reckoned with. It was a world where people lived close to the earth, themselves embedded within living, breathing nature; a time and place where our common distinctions between dream and reality, or nature and culture, had not yet fully emerged.

Now, with the birth of cities approximately 7500 BCE all this began to change as mythical thought would eventually give way to what we now call reason and rational reflection. In fact, as early as fifth century BCE Greece, the intellectual groundwork was already being laid and battle-lines drawn so that pre-Socratic philosophers — thinkers like Heraclitus of Ionia or Thales of Miletus — could begin making the final cut, separating nature *physis* (φύσις) from culture *nomos* (νόμος). Reflective of its cognate verb-root, *phyein*, meaning "to grow or develop," *physis* was understood in philosophic jargon of the day as that which occurs 'naturally' including that which is 'naturally' human. Nature, including human nature was in this view fundamentally opposed to *nomos* — that which was socially constructed by law, convention, or cultural circumstance. Such thinking provided early spadework for ideas later articulated by Sophists, arguing that laws (*nomoi*) are not natural (*physikos*), but simply a matter of convention, and thus relative — established through negotiation and agreed upon among people in specific communities at specific times. Nature (*physis*), on the other hand, was a given. In Plato's Protagoras, one of these sophists poses the tension as follows:

> *Gentlemen, he said, who are here*
> *present, I regard you all as kinsmen and*
> *intimates and fellow-citizens by nature,*
> *not by law: for like is akin to like by*
> *nature, whereas law, despot of mankind,*
> *often constrains us against nature."* (4)

With the Sophists, then, we see the fleshing-out of a conflict between custom and nature, and the concomitant position that laws (*nomoi*) are a product of social convention, an agreement among men fundamentally at odds with and, in large measure, encroaching upon our given nature (*physis*). Another Sophist went so far as to suggest that a truly 'ruthless individual' will naturally seek to escape the buoys of moral custom and the constraints of civil law. Or, as Antiphon put it, one may be prompted by nature to pursue only that which is in his own best interests, not necessarily what is lawful. (5)

According to these early debates, we can witness an antagonism emerging whereby the individual is uncomfortably pinned between a genuine Scylla and Charybdis — what's given to us by nature on the one hand and the civil demands imposed upon us by law or conventional norms on the other. We may rightfully surmise that such conventions are basically promulgated as a reactive response to the apparent exigencies of this all-too-human-nature, a nature needing to be constrained for the protection and benefit of society at large. So we see in these earliest struggles of Western tradition that an apparent conflict between *nomos* and *physis* would come to lie at the very foundation of civil society and the challenge of 'being good'.

Now, in the midst of such debates, we find Plato's own metaphysical meditations on the hierarchically organized tripartite human soul, where the rational element — trained by culture and moral convention, and aided by its higher spiritual dimension — rules over the lower, natural man... one's baser and insatiable animal desires. In short, we see that hypotheses were already being floated to validate the model of a hierarchically organized civil society, with its need to dominate and manage both nature and the body, including the body-politic, through establishment of a guiding civic moral order. (6)

Needless to say, throughout the ancient world, well into medieval times, and right up to the present day, ethical codes have been viewed as necessary, if not coercive correctives to the apparent egoism, self-interest, or concupiscence of human nature... the allegedly brutish instincts lodged within the folds of our flesh. While Freud made this a cornerstone of his work, Marshall Sahlins confirmed that the concept of "Original Sin pretty much sealed the deal in Christendom for centuries to come." (7) And as Elaine Pagels argued: "Augustine... offered an analysis of human nature that became, for better and worse, the heritage of all subsequent generations of Western Christians and a major influence on their psychological and political thinking." (8) So we understand that beginning with the Greeks and later, among the early Church Fathers, lay some of the essential theoretical groundwork for social and political philosophers in the West, including Enlightenment thinkers like Hobbes and Rousseau, themselves relying upon concepts already in the noosphere well before the time of Thucydides and the Peloponnesian Wars.

Even with his rather romantic view of pre-civilized humanity, Rousseau himself presumes this very same nature/culture divide — arguing in *The Social Contract* that the principal function of civil government is sublimation of the natural man in order to recreate him with a new 'moral' coat of armor. As Rousseau writes:

> *[The Legislator must] feel himself capable, so to speak, of changing human nature, transforming each individual, who is by himself a complete and solitary whole, into part of a greater whole from which that individual as it were gets his life and his being; weaken man's constitution to strengthen it; substitute a partial and moral existence for the physical and independent existence which we all have received from nature. (9)*

Obviously, this emergent, civilizing moral order was understood as anything but natural, looking rather like pure artifice, a construct of new forces producing citizens who could work and live together safely within well-defined city walls and an equally well-structured civil society. But, lost sight

of in such contrivance and civil convention — life's
fundamentally wild or unconstrained nature receded
further from view… apparently lurking just beneath
the surface, perhaps challenging civilization's
ability to maintain and control its well-ordered
cosmos. Even Rousseau himself recognized "it is no
light undertaking to separate what is original from
what is artificial in the nature of man". (10)
Einstein once offered a reflection that I believe
applicable to our current discussion of ethics.
"Mathematics," he notes, "are well and good but
nature keeps dragging us around by the nose". (11)
I would offer that his sentiment here applies equally
as well to ethics as it does to mathematics.

II.

It has been suggested by numerous scholars over
many decades — including researchers in paleo-
anthropology, archeology, ethnography, and
ethnology — that a fundamental key to human
survival throughout the millennia, and a primary
marker of the genus *Homo*, was our natural
sociability and the accompanying predisposition to
sharing of resources, whether that meant sharing
food from the hunt, tools for work, or even sexual

favors. (12) Our earliest forebears, living in small bands of pre-agricultural hunter-gatherers, shared anything and everything, including their thoughts: that is what distinguished them from most, if not all, of their primate cousins where dominance hierarchies and aggressive competition over food and mates held sway.

The capacity for *sharing*, it appears, was a primal and principally human activity central to continuance of our genus and species, while concurrently mitigating the need for political hierarchy. In fact, the reality of sharing militated against individual accumulation of power and control. Real political hierarchy, competition, and the hoarding of resources only emerged with the birth of cities on the heels of agriculture a mere six thousand years ago. But for the previous two hundred thousand years, Homo sapiens were largely egalitarian; and for approximately two million years prior, early representatives of our genus (*Homo erectus*) and later, *neanderthalensis*, also appeared to be egalitarian. Indeed, much of the available evidence suggests that *Erectus* socialized and shared food around campfires or open hearths, as did neanderthals nearly half a million years ago — the latter living in nuclear families, caring for their sick and elderly, and even burying their dead.

For most kinship-based cultures, the individual was constituted not only by his or her social relations within the tribe or band. In fact, there was apparently a deeper, intrinsic, and in a manner of speaking, an immaterial bond — we might even say a felt connective tissue — binding the community together. As M. Sahlins states:

> *Ethnographic reports speak of 'the transpersonal self' (Native America), of the self as a 'locus of shared social relations or shared biographies' (Caroline Islands) of persons as 'the plural and composite site of the relationships that produced them' (New Guinea). Referring broadly to the African concept of 'the individual,' Roger Bastide writes: 'He does not exist except to the extent he is outside and different from himself.' Clearly, the self in these societies is not synonymous with the bounded, unitary and autonomous individual as we know him. Rather the individual person is the locus of multiple other selves with*

*whom he or she is joined in mutual
relations of being...* (13)

Again, the individual in such a cosmos does not experience herself as an abstract, internalized, and isolated self, confronting or struggling against an objectified foreign world, or in competition with other egos there. Rather, the individual feels his or her existence only as an instantiation and structural component of the 'Other' — a necessary part of the banded community and intertwined with nature herself. As Sahlins continues:

*In kin relationships, others become
predicates of one's own existence, and vice
versa... It is the integration of certain
relationships, hence the participation of
certain others in one's own being. As
members of one another, kinsmen live each
other's lives and die each other's deaths...
[I]n kinship, as in relations to the cosmos
in general, alterity [the Other] is a
condition of the possibility of being.* (14)

I would suggest that there is a real sense here of what the anthropologist Lucien Levy-Bruhl has termed "participation mystique." (15) In our current context this may be described as a pre-conscious connection, indeed, a 'participation' of the Self in the Other, extending as well to the living cosmos — wherein human and non-human natures collide, co-mingle, and inter-animate one another. This sense of 'participation' — an immaterial connectivity among things — has been further illustrated in the literature, suggesting that our earliest forebears actively believed they could exercise influence over the natural world, as witnessed both through the reality of totemic identification as well as in the numerous examples of cave art depicting and summoning the desired game-animal before a hunt.

But if our most primal of ancestors literally could not fully separate themselves from tribe and totem, or separate the tribe and totem from their natural surround, then it may be more difficult to talk about self vs. world or nature vs. culture in respect to pre-civilized humanity. Rather, in this light, such distinctions do not yet exist, where the great variety of nature, including human nature, was seen as concrete manifestations of the same underlying power of being — what the indigenous Melanesians called *mana*, the Sioux Indians, *wakanda*, or the Iroquois, *orenda*.

If, in hunter-gatherer kinship bands, individuals participate one another, each and all together participating nature, why would not sharing and gifting be found at the very heart of tribal or banded communities, reflecting that primal experience of interconnectivity both among themselves and within their environment at large? In fact, that is precisely what we find as a defining characteristic of the earliest of pre-Neolithic economies. As Morton Fried states in his classic work, *The Evolution of Political Society*,

> *The paramount invention that led to*
> *human society was sharing because it*
> *underlay division of labor that probably*
> *increased early human productivity*
> *above the level of competitive species in*
> *the same ecological niches.* (16)

Elman Service confirms this in his own work on Primitive Social Organization: "The more primitive the society... the greater the emphasis on sharing, and the more scarce or needed the items the greater the sociability engendered." (17) As Tim Ingold concludes in his own work, The Perception of the Environment: It is more important "that food 'go around' rather than that it should 'last out'. Whatever food is available is distributed so that everyone has a share…" (18)

So, where does this leave us when confronted with the question of morality or the presumption of a purely self-regarding human nature that needs to be tamed through structural domination and hierarchical control? If social relations among our most primal ancestors were characterized by sharing, and sharing itself was based upon a felt inter-twining or 'participation-in-the-Other,' then we can be assured that such societies were organized along egalitarian lines, without obvious social ranking or economic stratification, save perhaps for the prestige that came with exceptional gifting. Fried confirms this:

Of almost equal importance [with sharing] was the concomitant reduction in the significance of individual dominance in a hierarchical arrangement within the community. In part, the structural possibility for such a hierarchy was undermined by the demands of sharing. [Even] cooperative labor parties… took place with little apparent leadership… (19)

So, is purely self-regarding behavior naturally human? Is there an evil human nature lurking just beneath our morally refined and civilized exterior? Or are thuggery, self-interest, and greed merely symptoms of modern culture and its relentless emphasis upon the individual — on competition, specialization, management and control, both of nature and our fellow man? As Sahlins concludes:

For the greater part of humankind, self-interest as we know it is unnatural in the normative sense: it [was] considered madness, witchcraft or some such grounds for ostracism, execution, or at least therapy. Rather than expressing a pre-social human nature, such avarice [was] generally taken for a loss of humanity. It puts in abeyance the mutual relationships of being that define a human existence. Yet if the self, the body, experience, pleasure, pain, agency and intentionality, even death itself, are transpersonal relationships in so many societies, and in all likelihood through so many eons of human history, it follows that the Western concept of man's self-regarding animal nature is an illusion of world-anthropological proportions. (20)

How then to make sense of our modern love affair with the emptiness of a 'me-first' society driven by self-serving and self-aggrandizing individuality? How do we properly understand or assess the unique habits and institutional arrangements of the Western-style, self-regarding morality of capitalism, of winner take all?

Perhaps Rousseau was correct when, in his rather romantic reconstruction in *The Origin of Inequality* he writes:

> *The first man who, having fenced in a piece of land, said 'This is mine,' and found people naïve enough to believe him, that man was the true founder of civil society. From how many crimes, wars, and murders, from how many horrors and misfortunes might not any one have saved mankind, by pulling up the stakes, or filling up the ditch, and crying to his fellows: Beware of listening to this impostor; you are undone if you once forget that the fruits of the earth belong to us all, and the earth itself to nobody.* (21)

Rousseau reminds us that the modern temperament willfully erased, in large measure, a more pristine capacity for egalitarian sharing. Losing sight of this foundational concern, we have sought to privatize, protect, and hoard whatever we can secure. Martin Heidegger acknowledges this primal loss in his *Introduction to Metaphysics*:

> *The fundamental error that underlies [the modern scientific temperament] is the opinion that the inception... is primitive and backward, clumsy and weak. The opposite is true. The inception is what is most uncanny and mightiest. What follows is not a development but flattening down as mere widening out... The uncanniest is what it is because it harbors such an inception in which, from over-abundance, everything breaks out at once into what is overwhelming.* (22)

Or, as Heraclitus states: "the limits of the soul cannot be surveyed, however broadly one strides, so deeply lies its ground." (23)

III.

If we reflect even briefly on the reality of our being
— that is to say, on human existence writ large —
we can easily feel ourselves already and always
engaged within the world, together with and
alongside other people there. Our own biology cries
out regarding our natural openness and participation
within the world. But, it is especially in human
community, that is, in our being-with-other-people,
that we may locate the real ground of ethical action.
As Hans Jonas wrote in his 1984 piece, *The
Imperative of Responsibility*: "ontology necessarily
entails a doctrine of obligation." So, while it may
not yet be completely evident, we may have
stumbled upon the linchpin of our natural capacity
for 'being good,' including our primal obligation to
Nature.

Seeking to get beneath an age-old tendency in
Western metaphysics, the philosopher, Martin
Heidegger, sought to describe human existence on
the far-side of any objectification, that is to say,
prior to any self-world dichotomy. He noted that
beginning with Greek philosophy after the pre-
Socratics there developed a pronounced tendency to

view our interactions within the world through one of the following lenses. The first lens is a more abstract or theoretical apprehension of things "present-at-hand," that is to say, objects to be observed or studied. The second lens is a view of things as "ready-to-hand," that is to say, our concrete and practical engagement with things as handy or useful for our projects and purposes. Yet, these lenses are both objectifying and presuppose a prior, more fundamental relationship to being. For example, as embodied, we always find ourselves embedded within a world in which we are already thrown and engaged. Heidegger calls this existential condition 'being-there' or, in the German, *Dasein* — considered as the foundational condition of human existence.

As Being-there, human existence displays its primordial openness; and this openness is not strictly biological. According to the philosopher — and prior to any objectification, manipulation or attitude of control — we naturally find ourselves "being-with-others." Our very nature as 'being-in-the-world' presupposes and implies our 'being-with' the Other even if there is no one else currently within earshot or in our field of vision. Other people serve, in part, to constitute my existence, much as I help constitute theirs. The existential reality of 'Being-with-the-other' reveals our fundamental inter-involvement with the world in which we are always, already engaged with other people there.

The term Care has been offered by Heidegger as the most effective way to describe, ontologically, this condition of openness which we naturally display towards other people. 'Being-with' grounds our fundamental care or concern for the Other as well as our responsibility towards one another. Here, then, we find a basis for Hans Jonas' assessment concerning ontological obligation. The very structure of our being, of our existence, implies a fundamental condition of availability to the Other (*Gelassenheit*), the mystery of our mutuality... not simply as an object "present-at-hand" or an instrument "ready-to-hand." Rather, we encounter the Other as another *Dasein*, another soul with whom we share not only the earth, but an essential connection as well. This, then, implicates us in a profound circle of reciprocity.

Literally thrown into the world with one another, we never find ourselves truly alone, floating in some alien universe. At the very least, there are always other people — filling our ears, troubling our hearts, or crossing our minds. In short, we find ourselves always, already engaged within a social milieu. Even when we are ostensibly alone and by ourselves, we are, strictly speaking, defined by the Other. But here things become rather interesting. If we understand ourselves always, already 'being-with-the-Other,' this fundamental or ontological co-inherence demands acknowledging that we are already pre-consciously involved with, connected to, concerned about, and in some respect, responsible for the Other. Care for the other is really built into the structure of our existence as 'being-with'. There is a primal connection, an intimacy between self and other, given with our very presence in the world.

And so, while moral codes may be relative to particular cultures at particular times, the fundamental relationship that defines human existence — our 'being-with-the-other' — prescribes a primal, ontological obligation vis-a-vis the Other. "Values," Jonas writes, "are more than just a matter of subjective choice." Well, there may be at least one obligation that derives from the nature of being itself. In other words, *Dasein's* very care structure — who we are fundamentally —

necessitates sharing as our most primary moral obligation.

IV.

Now, where has our inquiry taken us with respect to this fundamental question concerning the relationship between 'being' and 'being good,' or stated differently, between morality and our essential mortality? As Hans Jonas again reminds us, human beings are "free, but dependent; isolated, but in necessary contact..." (24) In short, we are by nature, that is to say, ontologically intertwined with the Other, dependent upon, and responsible to one another. So, ignoring for the moment those earlier claims that the foundation of the moral life rests with some kind of divine handiwork or revelation, like the stone tablets Moses purportedly brought down off the mountain to straighten-out the wandering Israelites; we must dig deeper, go beyond this remnant of any specific cultural memory. In short, we need to try and unearth what may have been existentially prior to, or underlying, such historical memories. We need to uncover the primal ground, that foundational modality of human-being wherein genuinely 'right' action is untethered from any specific religious or cultural commitment, as well as free from any sort of rational calculus or quid pro quo. Such thinking must not be instrumental, but rather meditative as the philosopher recommends. It is here that we turn our attention to the fundamental Care structure of human existence. Heidegger intentionally reminds us by way of recollecting a short fable recorded by Franz Bücheler, a myth that unveils for us the primal nature of Care, linked as it is to our future as well as our finitude — our earthly mortality.

> *Once when 'Care' was crossing a river,*
> *she saw some clay; she thoughtfully*
> *took a piece and began to shape it.*
> *While she was thinking about what she*
> *had made, Jupiter came by. 'Care'*
> *asked him to give it spirit, and this he*
> *gladly granted. But when she wanted*
> *her name to be bestowed upon it,*
> *Jupiter forbade this and demanded that*
> *it be given his name instead. While*
> *'Care' and Jupiter were arguing, Earth*
> *(Tellus) arose, and desired that her*
> *name be conferred upon the creature,*
> *since she had offered it part of her body.*
> *They asked Saturn to be the judge. And*
> *Saturn gave them the following*

decision, which seemed to be just:
"Since you, Jupiter, have given its spirit,
you should receive that spirit at death;
and since you, Earth, have given its
body, you shall receive its body. But
since 'Care' first shaped this creature,
she shall possess it as long as it lives.
And because there is a dispute among
you as to its name, let it be called
'homo,' for it is made out of humus
(earth)." (25)

What a delightful yet penetrating summary of our situation in the life-world! According to the myth, the being of *Dasein* — our being-there — is possessed by Care. That is how essential care is to human existence. It is within this Care-structure that human-being dwells... and in this dwelling is located the source of our concern for Others as well as our caring for and tending to the earth from which we were first given form.

As we come to grips with the finite nature of our existence, of our own mortality, we can't help but recognize this self-same frailty within the Other, as well as in the living cosmos that supports and sustains us. Recall the Greek term for 'nature' (*physis*) comes from the cognate verb *phyein*, meaning "to grow or develop," itself implying the other side of becoming, that is to say, death and decay. It is in this very recognition, I contend, that we find the source of our primary and constitutive moral obligation. As attested to in the fable, until the moment of death, our very being is possessed by Care, itself bodying-forth the "primordial structural totality" (26) of who we are — preceding any and every possible concrete 'attitude' we might hold or display, such as concern, solicitude, worry, or even carelessness. Again, Hans Jonas gives us a final reminder:

> *Life cannot at any time be imagined apart from its mortality… In the end, frailty of this existence is the very flip side of the sovereignty of its self-foundation… That life is mortal is indeed its fundamental contradiction, but this also belongs inseparably to its essence.* (27)

There is something about the nagging reality of death — about the finite nature of life, as Saturn justly pointed out — that calls for a special lucidity regarding how we should act in this world, a world filled with other frail living beings. It is in this very inseparability — of frailty and sovereignty — where we come face to face with our most pressing and primal moral imperative. It is the precariousness and vulnerability of life — the innate contradiction of a self which is no more than, and at the same time greater than its biology — that gives way, indeed, demands, our ongoing responsiveness and responsibility, not only for our own life, but for life writ large, and that means — for the Other in all its manifestations!

Notes:

(1) Mesopotamian Code of Urukagina from the City-State of Lagash, or the Code of Ur-Nammu also in ancient Sumeria (both ca. 2100 BC), or several hundred years later, the Babylonian Code of Hammurabi (ca. 1754 BC)

(2) Hans Jonas, *Memoirs*, 2008, p. 202

(3) Henri Frankfort, *Before Philosophy*, 1959, p.14

(4) Plato, *Protagoras*, 337c-d

(5) Diels-Kranz, 87 B44

(6) Plato, *Republic*, Book IV, 435d+

(7) Marshall Sahlins, *The Western Illusion of Human Nature*, 2011, p. 52

(8) Elaine Pagels, *Adam, Eve, and the Serpent*, Intro, p. xxvi

(9) Jean Jacques Rousseau, *The Social Contract*, Book 2, 7

(10) Jean Jacques Rousseau, *First and Second Discourses*, 93

(11) Anthony French, *Einstein, A Centenary Volume*, 1979

(12) Christopher Ryan, Cecilia Jetha, *Sex At Dawn*, 2010

(13) Marshall Sahlins, pp. 46-48

(14) Ibid

(15) Lucien Levy-Bruhl, *How Natives Think*, 1926

(16) Morton Fried, *Evolution of Political Society*, 1967 p. 106

(17) From Morton Fried, p. 106

(18) Tim Ingold, *The Perception of the Environment*, p.66

(19) Morton Fried, p. 106

(20) Marshall Sahlins, p.51

(21) Rousseau, *Discourse On The Origin of Inequality*, p.1

(22) Martin Heidegger, *Introduction to Metaphysics*, p.165

(23) Heraclitus, Fragment 45

(24) Hans Jonas, *Memoirs*, p. 230

(25) Martin Heidegger, *Being and Time*, p. 242. "Burdach has shown that the fable of Cura (which has come down to us as No. 220 of the Fables of Hyginus) was taken over from Herder by Goethe and worked up for the second part of his Faust. cr. especially pp. 40 ff. The text given above is taken from F. Bucheler (Rheinisches Museum, vol. 41, 1886, p. 5)" It is also interesting to note here that in astrology, Saturn signifies Justice.

(26) Martin Heidegger, *Being and Time*, p. 238

(27) Hans Jonas, *Memoirs*, p. 230

The Barbarian Within

By virtue of natality and the ability to act,
each new individual poses a threat to
civilization... The child carries barbarism
within him or her.
(Einar Overenget, *Hannah Arendt*)

Those tame and domesticated contours of civilized
life have all but eclipsed our sense of the 'feral' (the
wild, the untamed) in everyday experience — that
irrepressible anchor of embodiment, our original
interlacing with nature — 'that subtle knot which
makes us man' (Jon Donne, *The Ecstasy*) Ignoring
these roots, we've relinquished our original
freedom, just 'being-there' outside the terror of
historical consciousness. Abandoning this core
autonomy, the groundwork was laid for our own
enslavement to the irreversible march of civilization
and Father Time. But might we once again awaken
that primal experience, that natural sovereignty, and
recollect the untamed power of life-in-the-body-in-
the-world?

Okay! So now I hear the critics in the very back of
the room shouting: 'What the hell are you talking

about? Are you crazy? It was civilization that brought us freedom, brought us out of savagery, of slavery to the waywardness of nature's uncertainty!'

'Oh really?' I reply. 'You mean that agriculture — the spadework of civilization — was a liberating enterprise?'

Dare I disagree? In fact, farming required constant diligence, daily planning, control, and management of resources leading eventually to our own domestication, just as it led to domestication of the earth and the taming of other creatures here. This laid the foundations for our own enslavement, the polar opposite of freedom.

Neither was the birth of cities the actualization of real autonomy. To the contrary, urban life became a yoke around the neck of manager and laborer, landlord and tenant, legislator and citizen alike. Do we not now find ourselves preoccupied with the daily obligations of wage-slavery, ensuring the emptying of the present moment due to constant focus on an ever-receding future, a place where we plan release from our workaday drudgery? Is this not the direction of every modern polity, especially that propping up the American Dream?

I would argue that genuine self-rule emerges only by recollecting our primal ground — delivering us from subjugation to the demands of controlling institutional hierarchies, releasing us from the hypnotic attachment to some promised future, liberating us from the terror of history and the fear of death. This, however, requires overcoming that forgetfulness of our feral core.

In brief, we have become strangers to ourselves, reshaped by culture through epochal efforts in child rearing, training, and education. Yet to some degree we remain strangers to civilization because we have come to it from those wilder, primitive roots. Each individual bears within herself a certain surplus of being, an untamed nucleus that does not fit naturally (or comfortably) into domesticated patterns, and so can only be assimilated into a civilized milieu with great difficulty. This long forgotten undomesticated core represents our primary source of estrangement within the civil order. Yet, for most individuals, escaping alienation in order to recover some sense of liberation is at best an intellectual exercise or simply a romantic dream. But for others, for those whose civilized self has wholly papered-over their primal identity, such alienation can often reveal itself in nightmarish ways.

Recollecting this genetic memory-trace is key to breaking through the experience of alienation — an estrangement from nature, borne of one's cultural attachments and artfully constructed sense of self. In this way, the disaffection may become a gateway for rediscovering the underlying reality of the lived-body and its primal intimacy with nature. It can be a liberating event and a rebirth of spontaneity in the midst of everyday life.

Perhaps this is what sociologist Michael Epstein had in mind in *Transcultural Experiments* when he wrote of a tear in the fabric of civilized life, a glimpse of that inchoate and undomesticated heart that beats just beneath the surface of each citizen — a potentially haunting reminder of our ineluctable origin and our underlying engagement within the world.

So where is this liberating experience to be found in the midst of civilized life today? As I've learned, this memory-trace remains embedded deep within the flesh of every human being as a phylogenetic gift. It is a gift granting us the potential for episodic or periodic recovery of that primal integration of self and world. This memory-trace calls us back to the '*chiasm*' — that pre-reflective intertwining of body-as-subject and world-as-lived-by-my-body. But today this call seems accessible only by means of marginalizing experiences in a culture already made crazy by its own domesticating demands. This '*chiasm*' or breach finds voice in those culturally ambiguous circumstances where our normal frameworks come into question or simply no longer function properly — conditions that breed alienation and/or cultural ambiguity.

Whether such indeterminacy emerges in more private moments of extreme distress and euphoria, perhaps in the midst of nature, or in experiences like foreign travel, emigration, and cross-cultural exchange, a common thread seems to be the feeling of difference, of Otherness — either in the sense of 'being-beside' oneself, coping with the alterity of a strange world, of a stranger in our midst, or a growing awareness of the otherness of our own cultural perspective as Kurt Wolff wrote in *The Sociology of Georg Simmel*

.

> *The stranger [the Other], like the poor*
> *and sundry 'inner enemies,' is an*
> *element of the group itself. His position*
> *as a full-fledged member involves both*
> *being outside it and confronting it...*

It is here that alterity and strangeness become catalysts for more primal recollection because these are marginalizing experiences buried within each of us. Whenever we are confronted with marginality, have the feeling of being adrift without the safety and security of our cultural milieu (psychically, linguistically, or physically), it is in these moments or gaps that we may be struck by the uncultivated, untamed nature of life hiding just beneath the veneer of our well-worn artifices. Perhaps wherever we come face to face with our *facticity*, we may recover the experience of life as it once was and remains. Perhaps this is why the 'barbarian within' poses such a threat to civilized life, because a citizenry so exposed is difficult to control indeed.

It is in such *chiaroscuro* moments — at once clarifying and obscuring — that a schism, a breach, or fracture in our everyday world becomes a beacon pointing us back toward that subtle knot which makes us human. It is here that we may gather up the surplus of existence lying just beneath the surface of our civilized selves, finding our feral core in an act of retrieval, recovering the intimacy of a moment beyond historical consciousness, replacing us on a new path in the midst of the buzzing confusion of modern civilized life.

An American Foundation Myth

*The régime in Germany has betrayed you. Our
day of retribution has come.*

These remarks from Adolf Hitler's speech on March
2nd of 1933 appear in retrospect to be a disturbing
reminder as much as a fateful launching pad for
Donald Trump's own authoritarian mythology. At a
recent Conservative Political Action Conference,
our self-styled authoritarian relied on hauntingly
similar remarks as he sought to embolden his
followers with this declamation:

*I am your warrior. I am your justice. And
for those who have been wronged and
betrayed: I am your retribution.*

If this statement does not give one pause, it seems
clear, nevertheless, that such words are reminiscent
of Hannah Arendt's own assertion concerning the
'banality of evil.' In short, her turn of phrase almost
certainly defines the energy underlying Trump's
rhetoric as well as that animating his reactionary
and volatile base. As Arendt notes in her work on

Eichmann in Jerusalem, such evil emerges from a
failure of thought and then spreads "like a fungus."

> *Evil need not be committed only by
> demonic monsters . . . but by morons and
> imbeciles as well, especially if, as we see
> in our own day, their deeds are sanctioned
> by their religion.*

Not unlike Arendt's characterization of Eichmann,
Trump (our moron) is unable to imagine, let alone
inhabit, the viewpoint of the Other. And this makes
it virtually impossible for him to feel or admit that
what he does is wrong. Of course, this could explain
why he is incapable of uttering even a single word
or phrase that is not a self-serving cliche. And yet he
rambles tirelessly and without restraint. But, despite
his incapacity for genuine thought, this master of
the megaphone has become the spark igniting a
proven incendiary device, the radical Right and
their violent extremists. In the end, it is Trump's
reliance on the simple faith of these followers that
provides the leverage in promoting his anti-
democratic ambition. "Vengeance and retribution
are mine" concludes the author of *Deuteronomy*
(32:35). Again, the proximity to the former
President's thinking is more than a chilling

reminder of the roadmap being laid out for his followers and defenders of the faith.

Recent remarks emerging from the congressional conservative core — including from acolytes like Marjorie Taylor Greene, Lauren Boebert and others — continue echoing sentiments not dissimilar to the words expressed in Germany almost a century earlier. More to the point, the recent notoriety surrounding QAnon — that uniquely American millenarianist cult guided by the same presumption of White privilege embraced by its would-be savior — has thrust into the open undeniable elements of an underlying fascist eschatology. Nor is it surprising to find both blue and white-collar fundamentalists among Q's most ardent supporters, especially among evangelicals. In fact, this group of supporters appears to be an apocalyptic Christian nationalist movement demonstrating a pedigree harkening back as far as the New Testament's *Book of Revelation*.

Of course, for those like conservative representative Greene, Trump remains a 'once and future king,' an anointed savior, his executive role evidenced by fomenting a violent attack on our Capitol. With sticks and stones, body armor and battering rams, these cult followers sought to destroy those who would dare oppose Trump's divinely sanctified leadership. With perhaps a touch of irony, and not unlike Jesus' overturning the tables of the moneychangers at the Temple in Jerusalem, Trump unleashed his own legions on our temple of democracy to overturn a free and fair election. The symbolism here is thick and rich. Led by their would-be shaman decked out in horns and loin cloth, and animated by Trump acolytes, the insurrectionists hammered away at our Capitol as they continued hammering out elements of their own contemporary eschatological vision. With a special blend of Norse and Neo-Nazi themes, the insurrectionists literally sought to carve out their own mytho-historical reality, hoping to deliver on the promise of a new heaven and a new earth.

For the most part, these disgruntled insurrectionists spoke in a veiled tongue, a language laced with symbolism and metaphor. One key symbol — The Storm — served as placeholder for an apocalyptic event heralding the day of reckoning itself. This was to be that day when Trump's salvific return would explode across a national stage, and the infidels — those liberal blood-drinking pedophiles of the Deep State — would finally receive their divinely mandated retribution. Such sentiments bring us awfully close to an eschatological vision as we find it described in the *Revelation of Saint John the Divine* and his description of 'The Four Horsemen of the Apocalypse'.

> *I looked, and there before me was a white horse! Its rider held a bow, he was given a crown, and rode out as a conqueror bent on conquest. (6:2)*

> *Then another horse appeared, a fiery red one. Its rider was given power to take peace from the earth and have men slay one another. (6:4)*

> *I looked, and there before me was a black horse! Its rider was holding a pair of scales in his hand. (6:5)*

> *I looked and there before me was a pale horse! Its rider named Death, and Hades was following close behind him. (6:8)*

Surely these lines give us pause when considering the events surrounding that attempted insurrection on our Capitol. Again, the use of imagery and symbolism here is key, just as it was in St. John's apocalyptic vision. So perhaps, and by way of paraphrasing, it may not be too far-fetched to say the following of the former president's plan: Trump sought a crown for his head and, with a pair of scales in hand, he wished to ride out like a conqueror destroying the infidels, leaving only death and destruction in his wake.

It is no accident that the QAnon faithful remain steeped within an esoteric religious mythology. And, given their predisposition for apocalyptic eschatology, the energy of this cult is able to draw in millenarianists and extremists of all stripes, including white supremacists, Christian evangelicals, and many others factions in-between. Now, if we look back to the founding of our country, the roots of such behavior can be seen already percolating in the earliest stirrings of white privilege witnessed with the emergence of the American spirit centuries earlier. And now such nationalism has been unleashed through the progeny of those immigrants who first invaded the continent, decimating the native Americans already here inhabiting the land.

I would suggest in conclusion that the violence unleashed at our Capitol on that fateful day is merely the tip of an iceberg that is much bigger and has been growing for much longer than we may care to admit. Its origin is as old as those first pilgrims who set foot on this territory and the settlers who decimated indigenous inhabitants. In short, the mythologically infused movement of that seditious mob at the Capitol has been baked into the cake since before our founding just waiting to explode. I'm afraid to say that while we've already seen some of its fire and brimstone, the hot lava is about to engulf us. This uneasy, but not unlikely, alignment or political convergence of an apparently religious movement with a violent and broadly nationalist conspiracy appears to be leading us fast and furiously to an apocalyptic conclusion. And, while the myth itself is unnerving, the reality of its prospective realization is truly frightening.

A New Heaven and A New Earth:
On Myth, Madness, and Messianism

Proem

*Then I saw a new heaven and a new earth:
for the first heaven and the first earth were
passed away; and there was no more sea.
2 And I John saw the holy city, new
Jerusalem, coming down from God out of
heaven, prepared as a bride adorned for
her husband. 3 And I heard a great voice
out of heaven saying, Behold, the
tabernacle of God is with men, and he will
dwell with them, and they shall be his
people, and God himself shall be with them,
and be their God. 4 And God shall wipe
away all tears from their eyes; and there
shall be no more death, neither sorrow, nor
crying, neither shall there be any more
pain: for the former things are passed away.*
(1)

In these opening lines from chapter twenty-one of
the *Book of Revelation* we are made privy to the
Apostle John's rapturous vision of the new

Jerusalem, a 'holy city' coming down from heaven, the sins and sufferings of the flesh vanquished. By its very nature, the revelation is proleptic — that is to say, a vision of the eschaton or end time, signaling a return of the Messiah and the arrival of God's Kingdom on earth — the author speaking as if the kingdom is already upon us. Yet, such images require us to consider the philosophic and socio-political landscape currently haunting twenty-first century America and the madness loosed upon a largely unwitting citizenry by a decidedly sociopathic former president.

We are challenged to make sense of recent historical events by excavating the cacophony of voices that have apparently taken-hold of a large portion of our citizenry over these past several years — voices that have become more prominent as we glance back in the rearview mirror of a failed Trump presidential run. It is not enough simply to ignore or trivialize the messaging that has resulted; we need to find a way to understand what transpired, how it unfolded, and try to discover a reasonable path out of the madness and chaos it has unleashed.

There is a specter haunting America... reflecting the unique confluence of a peculiar kind of madness tethered to an unchecked messianism that has infected our politics. Such madness is a result of misguided assumptions and mythological narratives that have unfortunately but gravely poisoned what passes for current political discourse. Of course, we are not alone in recognizing the madness that undergirds 'civil' discourse today; Sigmund Freud, Eric Fromm, R. D. Laing, and Paul Shepard are among a host of thinkers who have offered their own critiques of Western civilization in these terms. Yet, there is a very specific malady currently afflicting a large segment of the American public along with some of their elected representatives. It is from this vantage point that we propose to examine the machinations of this phantasm and try to uncover some sense as to where the national psyche currently rests or where it might be headed.

Myth

In this inquiry, mythology appears as both primal and primary. The language of myth —whether dressed up as a biblical story, quaint fable, or perhaps in some other oral or written narrative — provides a visceral response to existential issues that otherwise need to find a voice. In this manner, myth helps illuminate a community's self-understanding, providing a specific window on the collective and its relationship to their life-world. As Hans Jonas writes in his *Memoirs*,

> *When it comes to certain questions, Plato tells us, philosophical Logos has nothing to say, while myth has the ability to speak of them metaphorically.* (2)

Unfortunately today, the most common view of myth is also its most simplistic and, to that extent, grossly off the mark. In common parlance, the term 'myth' has often been used pejoratively to indicate that some apparent statement of fact or some point of view is plainly false or unverifiable. 'Oh... that's just a myth' or, its equivalent, 'that's an old wives tale' might be a common refrain. Obviously this is not how we are using the term within the current context.

Myth and the activity of myth-making stem from some of the earliest stirrings of human creativity — along with carved Venus figurines, primitive cave drawings, or other archaic artifacts, including sacred narratives such as we find in the Old and New Testaments. Throughout human history and

101

prehistory, mythic heroes have provided a grounding faith, connecting people to their community as well as the surrounding environment. In this respect I regard myth as sacred history.

Not a few researchers have suggested that myth works through the embodiment of forces animating cultural memory. By articulating the power that both enlivens and sustains one's life-world, myth provides both individual and community a way to grasp the significance of current events, placing them within a foundational context. Myth serves in this capacity by joining present reality to otherwise primeval events and, through the narrative form, allows those in the present to partake in a special status accorded to a time of origins. In this respect, myth serves to anchor present action within a meaningful and primal framework.

Given their fundamental existential bearing, the elements of any myth may also be adapted and/or interpreted as applying to a broad array of current social or historical events, thereby bestowing a special status upon otherwise apparently mundane affairs. Just as we can demythologize primal mythic events, thereby disclosing some underlying existential sense, so too can historical personages or events become the subject of myth — themselves being mythologized, thereby bestowing a special sacred status or legitimacy by means of the mythic narration. This process of mythologizing can be found in some of the earliest of narratives of civilization, for example, in the Mesopotamian *Epic of Gilgamesh* or the mytho-historical narratives concerning the early God-kings of ancient Egypt.

Here I agree with Jan Assmann when he asserts that in myth there is a natural intertwining of "foundational" and "biographical" elements.

> *One might even say that cultural memory transforms factual into remembered history, thus turning it into myth. Myth is foundational history that is narrated in order to illuminate the present from the standpoint of its origin.* (3)

Considering this concept of myth and myth-making, we might redirect our attention briefly to the early pre-history of our species. Members of our genus have roamed the earth for nearly two million years, and *Homo sapiens* for some 200,0000 years. As for our sub-species, *Homo sapiens-sapiens*, we have been around for roughly 35,000 years. All of this was well before history or the birth of civilization a mere 6,000 years ago along the Fertile Crescent in the ancient Near-East at the confluence of the Tigris-Euphrates River Valley. Scholars have suggested that the earliest members of our species, genetically like us, experienced the world quite differently than we do today. As French sociologist and anthropologist, Lucien Levy-Bruhl, wrote:

While pre-civilized peoples saw with eyes like ours, they may not have perceived the world with the same minds. (4)

On its face, the statement seems startling. What could it mean to say that earlier members of our species may have perceived the world with a different mind? And if we take the statement at face value — that early humans did not perceive with the same minds as us — then surely the world they perceived must have been qualitatively different; in other words, this world... but differently constituted! But, what does a statement like this imply about objective reality? Well, at the very least, it suggests that what we perceive is in part a function of our subjective experience, not only in the sense of our particular location in time or space, but our state of mind as well. That is to say, what we perceive depends in some significant measure on the presuppositions or predispositions that create our perspective most broadly conceived.

Now, considering the pre-history of our species and the experience of our primitive forebears, I wager that their perception of the natural world (the surrounding environment) was in some substantive way constituted differently than our perceptions today. We might even agree that our pre-civilized ancestors did see with different minds. In fact, more than a few researchers have argued this very point. But, what exactly might have constituted the nature of that difference?

It has been argued that our earliest predecessors were bound together not simply through totemic connections, but rather, (and this is what totemism ultimately implied) they felt this connection by means of a pervasive but somewhat inarticulable experience of power. This experience has been given various names among diverse indigenous populations, including *mana* among Melanesians, *hasina* in Madagascar, *vaki* among the Baltic Finns, *orenda* among the Iroquois Indians, or *wakanda* with the Sioux. These are among some of the most primeval predications of power undergirding and giving life to the myth-making experience. (5)

Now, this view is typically labelled 'primitive animism' — a belief that the world is alive, drenched in a medium of power. Anthropologist, Lucien Levy-Bruhl called this experience 'participation mystique' — the intuition of an elemental force which, though largely supra-sensible, is nevertheless real and connecting individuals fundamentally to the surrounding environment. (6) This was a world bathed in power, where even a simple cave drawing or utterance could magically impact reality. Nature itself was in this sense peopled, not with mere objects-at-hand, but with real subjectivities responsive to human coaxing or cajoling. All early religious sentiment had its roots in this mythic experience of power. This is what the Egyptologist, Henri Frankfort, meant when he wrote in *Kingship and the Gods*:

> *The creations of the primitive mind are elusive. Its concepts seem ill-defined, or, rather, they defy limitations. Every relationship becomes a sharing of essentials. The part partakes of the whole, the name [partakes] of the person, the shadow and effigy of the original. This 'mystic*

participation' reduces the significance of distinctions while increasing every resemblance. It offends all our habits of thought. Consequently, the instrument of our thought, our language, is not well suited to describe primitive conceptions. (7)

This kernel of the myth-making experience — that extraordinary power underpinning everyday reality — was present not only within the world of primitive and early civilized cultures, but lingers on, enlivening our own spiritual traditions, religious institutions and intuitions as well as the sacred histories grounding our most sacrosanct socio-political arrangements. Myth was, and still is, a natural response to the preternatural experience of power, of engagement, of an indefinite but profound sense that there is 'something going on here' that is not adequately understood or grasped in terms of pure reason — that is to say, rationally, scientifically. In this way, myth becomes the principal medium through which that experience finds expression. Such articulation surrounds those who make the myths as well as those who are absorbed by them.

This is in part what we may be experiencing today around the strangest of all carnival barkers — the former president, Donald Trump. He has been cast in the role of a mythic hero as well as myth-maker among a specific contingent of our citizenry. In this regard, he is seen by his followers as one who can alter, change, or remake world history. Again, myth-making is a primal and natural response to the experience of power wherever it shows itself. And we see how the clearly autocratic stylings of this twice-impeached former president, together with his rather incoherent Caligula-like ramblings — "Remember that I have the right to do anything to anybody" (8) or alternatively "I am your retribution" — make quite an impression. Trump certainly sounds like a narcissistic megalomaniac, and such statements may rightfully engender the stuff of myth-making and hero worship.

The Caligula reference is quite on point. Similarities concerning the madness shared by these two world-historical figures is frightening. Indeed, part of Trump's lure — ignorance of policy and dictatorial style rising to mythic stature — is his concretization of a power capable of creating its own reality. Here we must investigate the meaning of that madness and its accession to power in America today. Madness

In his 1967 publication, The Politics of Experience, visionary Scottish psychiatrist R. D. Laing, voiced what at the time seemed almost an absurd idea — that madness, however one defines it, is only 'mad' when considered from the perspective of a mad society which forms its 'normal' social reality. Well, perhaps Laing was right; just maybe the 'madness' that underlies and sustains our current societal reality is beginning to ooze out of the woodwork, showing itself not only around the brittle edges of life, but spilling over right there onto the cutting-room floor. So perhaps it is not a stretch in suggesting that our former president and his ecstatic entourage are showing real signs of a specific kind of madness that has been propping up American society? As Adam Garfinkle, writing in *The American Interest*, concludes…

> *[Trump is a] narcissist of such extreme qualities that he is in many respects its quintessence. It is therefore hardly surprising that he appeals to so many others wandering around lost in the same set of funhouse mirrors. Trump has managed to turn himself into a Ripley's Believe It or Not-style carnival barker and its main attraction at the same time — not obviously fictive but not matter-of-factly*

real either. Not even P. T. Barnum achieved
that feat of attention-grabbing mesmerization,
that transformation of spectacle into political
capital. (9)

In short, Trump has managed to emerge not only as
an ersatz mythological figure — a venerated hero to
his berserk following — but also as genuinely
disturbed, trumpeting his less-than-heroic
accomplishments and bold-face lies to a cadre of
sociopathic followers day-in and day-out. In fact, as
the journalist, Shane Snow, noted in his February
15, 2017 post in the online platform, *Medium*, most
professionals now view the former president as a
'malignant narcissist' — a concept first coined by
social psychologist, Erich Fromm, in his 1964 work,
The Heart of Man. And, as psychologist John
Gartner clarifies, Fromm's concept covers those
individuals with anti-social, paranoid, and
narcissistic personality disorders all rolled up
together into one formidable disease. And our boy,
Trump, certainly seems to fit the bill.

But no matter what the specific nature of the malady
afflicting this former president, it is just the tip of a
much larger iceberg that is emerging. The real
concern is not so much Trump himself, whose

110

illness has been clearly visible in daily statements and behaviors. Our more urgent concern is those signs of illness that are more markedly showing themselves in the behavior of a majority of the Republican party faithful starting with the QAnon loyalists themselves. Not unlike earlier followers of false prophets — self-deluded, and perhaps self-medicated — these folks feel themselves enlivened, emboldened, and enlightened. And that is the heart of our current troubles, a real heart of darkness lurking on the fringes of our society and threatening to become mainstream, if not more violent; and it is already infecting members of Congress.

The simmering madness that is fast enveloping our nation is clearly evident in a corrupt and distorted view of reality, a ready acceptance of unproven claims, as well as a real distain for non-believers of the fantasy. The nature of the illness, compounded by the strength of its wild convictions, has followers believing that they are normal and the rest of us are either evil, sick, or both. And therein lies the heart of our national crisis.

A not-insignificant portion of America's adult population is blindly marching arm-in-arm with a 'malignant narcissist.' Unaware of their own

compromised condition, these true believers feel
that the problem is not their own but our's. And, not
unlike the story of Don Quixote, they follow their
leader around as he continues tilting at windmills.
Unfortunately, our most pressing national affliction
is no longer a Corona virus, but the insanity of
beliefs and actions taken on the basis of absurdities.

Messianism

In January of 2021 middle-class Navy veteran Jacob
Anthony Chansley, a bare chested, self-proclaimed
fur-trim and horned QAnon shaman, rose up much
like a would-be biblical prophet-of-old intent on
leading a violent gang of insurrectionists inside the
United States Capitol to face off against 'enemies'
of their mythic hero, then-president Donald Trump.

Now, as outsiders par excellence, shamans occupy
what Victor Turner has called a 'liminal' space,
typically located at the outermost edge of a
community. Often called to this unique profession
unwillingly, and after undergoing a variety of
disturbing trials or initiatory experiences, shamans
learn to deal with both spirits of nature and other

preternatural forces to address a community's hardships and protect the well-being of its members.

Our so-called QAnon shaman belonged to no such community. And while he claimed to have defeated 'dark demonic forces', it is evident that Chansley himself has never undergone any real initiatory experiences or spiritual trials. And, while he does appear delusional — most likely from being self-medicated — he is no more than a wandering minstrel with little more to show for himself than his horned headdress and some ragged tattoos in the folds of his flesh. He was, for all intents and purposes, not a shaman, but a sham. Be that as it may, he enjoyed making proclamations and taking action on behalf of the former president.

According to Chansley's own statements on Facebook, this wanna-be new-age prophet saw himself as some kind of 'metaphysical warrior' or 'compassionate healer'. A self-described 'con-spiritualist' (something at the intersection of conspiracy theorist and New Age mystic), Chansley was apparently convinced that a second Trump term would usher in a new world order — 'a new heaven and a new earth' — perhaps something akin to the

Ascension of Christ, the Great Awakening, or a biblical rapture.

It could be argued that Chansley was acting under the influence of mythological thinking. In any event, this self-proclaimed shaman was apparently prepared to capture and/or assassinate elected government officials in order to consummate his apocalyptic vision and usher in the new age. Indeed, many of the insurrectionists following his lead held tight to the conviction that a battle — **Coming Storm** — would ensue between the forces of light and the forces of darkness. According to one journalist's summation...

> *[A] biblical rapture of sorts or 'storm' would rain down on the country during the inauguration at noon on Wednesday - when forces amassed by Trump would... arrest Biden and other Democrats on live TV while Trump would be sworn in for a second term.* (10)

In view of this mythic scenario, let us look at another phenomenon that may help shed light on the situation. In his classic study of cargo cults, *The Trumpet Shall Sound*, British sociologist Peter

Worsley offered a summary of this primitive Melanesian phenomenon.

> *[In these] strange religious movements… a prophet announces the imminence of the end of the world in a cataclysm which will destroy everything. Then the ancestors will return, or God, or some other liberating power, will appear, bringing all the goods the people desire, and ushering in a reign of eternal bliss* (11).

Such a description reminds us of the apocalyptic intention evident in our would-be prophet, Chansley, and his savior-figure, Donald Trump.

Now Worsley further qualifies these cults as messianic millenarian movements bent on prosecuting an agenda of social unrest and heralding the end-time… a genuinely proleptic anticipation of an apocalyptic end of the old and the arrival of a new glorious world order. And it seems that our QAnon followers, along with their self-proclaimed shaman, were in fact awaiting just such salvation from their cult savior along with a few of his acolytes.

As Lamont Lindstrom wrote in *The Cambridge Encyclopedia of Anthropology*: while ethnographers have noted that the term 'cargo' originally referred to highly sought-after Western commercial goods, it just as easily signaled an "expectation of moral salvation, existential respect, or proto-nationalistic, anti-colonial desire for political autonomy". (12) The term 'cargo cult' thus became synonymous with any social movement aspiring to renewed religious or political relevance. As Mike Davis wrote in 2017, "The Great God Trump and the White Working Class,"

> *The millenarian aspects of the Trump campaign — the magical nativism and promise of a world restored — have received surprisingly little comment although together with his erratic ravings they were perhaps its most striking features.* (13)

As I am suggesting, the QAnon crowd showed some real signs of just such a modern-day cargo cult, believing that the end-time is near, that an apocalyptic moment is at hand. And under Trump's leadership, this is what precipitated the attack on the U. S. Capitol — an event whose teleological intention was clear, the ushering in of a new age with Trump as their "cargo prophet."

The quasi-nativistic and presumed spiritual nature of QAnon as a modern cargo-cult now raises basic questions regarding the proto-religious dimension of this political movement along with its associated beliefs. And this brings us again directly to the issue of their self-proclaimed shaman. But to grasp this correctly, let's first consider shamanism in its pristine form among archaic and traditional cultures.

As we can well imagine, shamanism is a tricky concept to pin down because it has been used in so very many different contexts. And such conceptual complexity often serves to confuse understanding of the authentic phenomenon. But at its core, we can say that shamanism refers to magico-religious or proto-religious phenomena found originally among Neolithic societies and other indigenous cultures. According to historian of religion, Mircea Eliade:

> *It is generally agreed that shamanism originated among hunting-and-gathering cultures, and that it persisted within some herding and farming societies after the origins of agriculture. It is often found in*

117

conjunction with animism, a belief system
in which the world is home to a plethora of
spirit-beings that may help or hinder
human endeavors. (16)

The social role of the shaman is generally held to be continuous with older forms of magico-religious practice dating back as early as the late Paleolithic. Since the beginning of the twentieth century, ethnologists and anthropologists have used the terms shaman, medicine-man, sorcerer, witch-doctor, and magician somewhat interchangeably, denoting those possessing special healing or sacred powers found in nearly all traditional societies. Furthermore, the same term has been nominally applied in describing similarly religious phenomena among civilized peoples as well. In this respect we find discussions of Indian, Iranian, German, Chinese, even Babylonian shamanism.

Despite some modern attempts to romanticize and popularize shamanism, those who are 'chosen' seldom have an easy time of it. Many are called to their vocation through near-death experiences, spiritual crises and other terrifying and harrowing rites of passage. (17)

As well, entering a state of ecstatic trance was always part and parcel of the shaman's vocation. And while we can find cases of shamans leading groups into battle, traditionally, the shaman was healer and medicine man, maintaining the health of the community. But the shaman also served as *psychopomp* — conducting the souls of the dead safely into the afterlife.

Unfortunately in the USA today, shamanism has become just another new age or avant-garde spiritual phenomenon, replacing Buddhism as the hot religious practice of the twenty-first century. As a matter of fact, one can even sign-up online for a 60-minute workshop to become 'certified'. This might be the same place Mr. Chansley received his own shamanic license.

By means of his divine madness, the shaman functions as healer, prophet, and custodian of sacred traditions — working to insure maintenance of cultural harmony and the continuity of society. But, apparently our QAnon shaman never got the message or really did not understand his role. Chansley and his cohort seemed determined to do the opposite — overturning the social order and trying to destroy our cultural and political integrity.

In short, it seems as though a growing lunatic-fringe of the 'biblical wing' of the Republican Party has taken increasing control of the Right's entire political message. The essence of that message over two years ago, was that Donald Trump, like an angel of the Lord, will come back into power and, after mounting a final attack on those infidel Democrat elitists, be reinstated to his rightful throne in Washington.

A Not So Tactful Conclusion

As I have sought to clarify, there is a disconcerting psychopathology propping up American culture today; it is a malady so insidious that we find a plurality of citizens believing in the mythic-heroic stature of a disgraced former president — an out of touch madman, devoid of empathy, tact, or genuine concern for anyone but himself. Such a malady has led far too many of our compatriots to embrace this messianic myth in the first place, finding its most vociferous adherents among white Christian evangelicals and the dispossessed. In concert with a ragtag gang of once-and-future insurrectionists, these true believers seem dead set on eclipsing our democracy in the hopes of bearing witness to the unfolding of their own deluded narrative — the dawning of a new heaven and a new earth. So, it is no surprise that they are positioned at the forefront of this political charade. Nor is it shocking to find that the faithful — hoping to usher in a divine kingdom ruled over by Trump's iron fist — have made common cause with those who would hasten a revolutionary revolt and the resulting social upheaval.

We must not forget that anticipation of this new dawn, where death will be vanquished, harbors within itself an underlying distain, not just for the body politic, but for the physical body as well — practically dismissing the concrete ways in which we both touch and are touched by one another through empathy, tact, and yes, even physical intimacy. (18) And according to this fundamentalist Christian myth, we should no longer have a need for our bodies in any event. But, lest they forget, the *Gospel of John* clearly reminds us that the Word in fact became flesh in the very body of their beloved savior! We need also remember that our ability to touch and be touched is what allows for genuine empathy in the first place; and a society that loses touch with the flesh loses touch with itself. (19)

But, perhaps we have already lost touch, not only with ourselves but with our ability to touch or be touched by the another. If so, can we really find a way back into our senses and once again be touched by our world? In fact, that may be our only hope in bringing an end this apparently unyielding and unbearable madness threatening to engulf us.

Notes

(1) *Book of Revelations*, Chapter 21

(2) Hans Jonas, *Memoirs*, p. 216

(3) Jan Assmann, *Cultural Memory and Early Civilization*, p. 37, 38

(4) Lucien Levy-Bruhl, *How Natives Think*

(5) Ernst Cassirer, *Language and Myth*, p. 66

(6) Lucien Levy-Bruhl, Ibid

(7) Henri Frankfort, *Kingship and the Gods*, p. vii

(8) From Suetonius, Roman Historian

(9) Adam Garfinkle, 'The Present Madness' June 15, 2020

(10) Samson Amore, January 20, 2021 *The Wrap*

(11) Peter Worsley, *The Trumpet Shall Sound*, 1957

(12) L. Lindstrom, *The Cambridge Encyclopedia of Anthropology*

(13) Mike Davis, 'The Great God Trump and White Working Class'

(14) *Genesi*s 19:24

(15) Mircea Eliade, *Shamanism*, Bollingen, 1964

(16) Ibid

(17) Valerie Taliman, 'Lakota Declaration of War,' 1993

(18) Richard Kearney, *Touch*, Columbia, 2021, pp. 45-52

(19) Ibid, p. 47

Breaking America's Social Architecture

ONCE UPON A TIME in America, citizens had an abiding faith in the strength of their mutual relations — what I will call the 'social architecture' of community. These relationships provided an ability to engage one another within a relatively stable civic environment. Under those conditions the American Dream was alive and well, and running rather smoothly over some well-worn tracks. Such civic engagement was reflected by widespread participation in all manner of public association, including religious congregations, trade unions, chambers of commerce, humanitarian service clubs like Rotary, Lions, and the Kiwanis, as well a host of other broad-based community organizations.

It is important to note that the word 'community' derives from two rather ancient Latin roots — *cum* and *munus*; loosely translated it means "to give or share with one another." Yet, perhaps this definition seems rather quaint in today's increasingly competitive environment, in a world where *communio* or 'sharing' suddenly feels more like 'giving something up' or 'giving it away'. Still, as a youth growing up in the late 1950s and early 1960s,

I found the evident security provided by community created a safe haven for the enjoyment of everyday life. Simple faith in my community provided a sense of the world and a worldview that was anchored and unshakable. However, as I grew, such assurances seemed to evaporate like hot steam on a cold mirror. Concurrently, the stabilizing effects of *communitas* slowly began eroding, revealing that this initial faith was perhaps naive. The loss of faith in community has shown that, while people can behave in surprisingly harmonious ways when joined together communicating or collaborating, it also reveals the potential dissonance or madness of the crowd as well.

In his 1970 article published by *The New Yorker* magazine, Charles Reich — a principal proponent of the '60s counterculture movement and author of *The Greening of America* — put into rather stark relief what appeared an emergent challenge to the 'social architecture' on whose ground several generations of Americans were nurtured and raised.

As he wrote at the time:

> *There is a revolution underway. It is not like revolutions of the past. It has originated with*

the individual and with culture, and if it
succeeds it will change the political structure
only as its final act. It will not require violence
to succeed, and it cannot be successfully
resisted by violence. It is now spreading with
amazing rapidity, and already our laws,
institutions, and social structures are changing
in consequence. Its ultimate creation could be
a higher reason, a more human community,
and a new and liberated individual. This is the
revolution of the new generation.

While the influence of Reich's revolutionary call should not be minimized, I must also note that he was heralding a revolution without violence; it was a call for cultural revolution aimed at addressing the issues of personal freedom, political equality, and the direction of civic life. So, while the foundations of our social architecture were under question, Reich was calling us not to bear arms against one another but rather to engage in debate and dialogue — a collective reassessment of the country's social architecture. In short, he sought expanded the nature of communication within community.

Now let us fast-forward to the present day, to the America of a post-Trump presidency. We all watched in amazement and horror on that infamous day while the political grounding of our social architecture was literally being ripped from its moorings by violence; it was an attempt to overthrow our very system of governance. While Reich's *Greening*, and its consciousness-raising revolution of the 1970s, was a cultural rebellion aimed principally at the Corporate State, this new insurgency was now attacking us not only in city streets but in election boards, governors' offices, and courthouses — including the Supreme Court. It was a different creature altogether. This new insurgency was an oddly authoritarian intrusion emerging from within a specific segment of the body politic itself, and giving rise to a host of conspiratorial movements.

The rise of groups like QAnon, the Proud Boys, Oath Keepers as well as other militaristic or neofascist ideologies, is more than a cautionary tale. According to the Public Religion Research Institute findings earlier this year, nearly 20% of Americans and 25% of Republicans believe in one or more of the QAnon conspiracies. Furthermore, QAnon congressional candidates were on the ballot in at least twenty-six states as of April 2022. But this is only the tip of an iceberg that is expanding as it

seeks to undermine our commitment to social amity,
democratic process, and finally, rationale thought.

We must now consider a few critical issues. Is it
already too late to coax these mythologically driven
reactionaries to engage in some form of reasoned
debate; or, has their blind faith in the myth — still
tethered to an aggressive neofascist ideology —
eclipsed their capacity for discussion and reasoned
engagement? Apparently the insurgents have no
desire for dialogue or debate. Rather, and in
partnership with their far-right-leaning
congressional sponsors, they seek hand to hand
combat instead. They want to disrupt and ultimately
transform an otherwise reasonable socio-political
structure into an autocratic religiously driven
ideology.

So what should we now expect? What avenues
remain open for meaningful action that may repair
or heal our fast-crumbling social reality? I'm afraid
there may not be too many more options available,
nor the possibility of achieving very much — unless
and until we elect politicians blessed with both
reason and a genuine capacity for grounded moral
judgement. By this, I do not simply mean electing
Democrats, but Republicans and Independents as

well, anyone who shares our interest in leading both a political and legal movement to protect this country against the threat of an autocratic theocracy. If not, we may be condemned — much like Sisyphus in the myth — to rolling a boulder up the mountain, only to have it tumble back to the bottom each and every time.

Embodiment, Ecstasy, Emptiness
~ the Alchemy of Wonder

Altai State Pedagogical University, Barnaul, Russia, April 2021

The legacy of civilization suggests an irredeemable obsession for control of both external and internal reality, and the need to extend that control wherever possible — environmentally, socially, politically, economically, and psychologically. This overriding drive for command and control was given full-throated foundation by Aristotle with the articulation of a simple tool of logic called the syllogism: If A=B and B=C then A=C. Syllogistic reasoning led inevitably to the 'discovery' of laws allowing for more efficient control of nature, as well as the enactment of social laws to better control human behavior. The syllogism thus lay at the very heart of the civilizing project in both the natural and the human sciences — a headlong pursuit to dominate nature, and a never-ending battle for dominion over our fellow man.

The spectacular unfolding of historical consciousness that had already shown itself with the first stirrings of urban life in the ancient Near-East nearly six thousand years ago triggered an unrelenting drive to understand the past in order to direct the course of the future,

130

providing the underlying narrative of modern life. In short, we were born into a world to be managed — going back as far as the Neolithic period when mankind first gave up the nomadic life of hunting and gathering and began to farm the earth instead.

But the uncertainties borne of historical consciousness, including agriculture and urbanization, were substantive. Indeed, the planting of crops necessitated waiting; which itself led to anxiety over the future — the desperate need for control fully emerged in that fateful moment. Worrying about the future continued to occupy human thought with the early Israelite belief in a transcendent deity's promise to his chosen people. And, the hope for a future of salvation would be more fully fleshed-out down through the early centuries, including the diverse canons of religion, politics, science, and technology.

Just look around, the signs and symbols of control are everywhere. They reside in your smart-phone, on your laptop, in your calendar, on your watches and in your time clocks. Control can be found on the evening news, in your finances, or just sitting in your doctor's office waiting. But that is not all. In addition to forecasting, we also want to manipulate the weather, bend it to our demands, our desires, and our military campaigns. We push without respite to control all that is wild and

131

untamed, domesticating every centimeter of nature, including our own inclination to shun those hierarchies constraining us.

Control is present in our news leaks, in our military hardware, in sales forecasts, and commercial advertising. Control oozes out from your insurance policies and finds voice in your bank deposits; it is the assumed authority brandished among the police, the lawyers, and the judges; it runs like a vein of fools-gold throughout the army, the navy, and the air force; it is built into the principles of management and leadership — planning, scheduling, and the assignment of work; everything we do is about control. The very institutions and hierarchies we have erected are the embodiment of this singular and overriding obsession.

One could argue that this preoccupation with control is not a modern phenomenon; one could suggest that our Pleistocene forebears sought the comfort and certainty of a control as well. Some might argue that we can find this in a simple review of early hunting practices, shamanic ritual, or evidence of a belief in magic in the early Neolithic. However, I would simply note that if there appears to us moderns the telltale signs of pre-civilized magic (to influence the hunt for example), perhaps such practices could be interpreted in other ways, and not necessarily as attempts to manage outcomes as understood today. Needless to say, such practices would have been minimally invasive to the natural workings of the cosmos in comparison to our satellite-directed drones or our hell-fire missiles, our enforced economic servitude or our nuclear power-plants. In any event, our pre-civilized forbears certainly fit into their landscape far better than we do today.

Even the medieval alchemist did not seek control over nature as we understand it, but rather a balance among various elements in order to achieve a higher order harmony. But we have done the opposite — trying to exercise so much control that experts readily predict 'imminent and irreversible planetary collapse.' The most absurd of ironies rests in this fact: that the struggle for predominance (control of nature) has led to the most untenable and uncontrollable circumstance one could have imagined. Rather than perfecting our relationship with nature, we have driven the planet and ourselves to the unmanageable brink of global disaster. So what are we to do? How are we to overcome the insurmountable obstacles we have placed in our own way?

Of course, various proposals may be floated to address such a crisis; more often than not they rest upon being proactive, taking action. We always seem to be working diligently to solve problems we've created. Yet, such activity typically leads into the same trap as the methodology that created our problem in the first place. The response always assumes the right of dominion, of self-determination, an anthropocentric view of the world. But, which is more quixotic, tilting at windmills or building them in order to escape our chosen fate by producing electricity in a new way? So let us now switch gears and examine another way.

The Chinese concept of *Wei wu wei* represents the Taoist ideal of acting through non-action, sometimes called 'effortless action'. Of course this sounds like a contradiction in terms; however, it is really about overcoming our obsession with control and manipulation, domination and dominion. *Wei wu wei* suggests abandoning the incessant pull on our energies, the will to direct all activity or define all outcomes. It is about openness, spontaneity, and yes… letting go; it is something I myself struggle with daily! Yet, this same ancient Taoist idea is reflected conceptually in the later writings of German philosopher Martin Heidegger. The term Heidegger uses is *gellasenheit*. In the philosopher's jargon, this refers to a state of 'openness' or, as he calls it, 'releasement,' an unwillingness to control or define outcomes — a mode of non-interference with the natural flow of life's energy. It is a turning away from the will and willing; rather, it is a 'non-willing' or 'letting-be'. In such a posture one may experience the world not simply as a series of objects for manipulation and control, but, rather as an open horizon. It is a receptive posture, rather than aggressive. In this manner, it allows that which is in front of us to show itself. This is a posture where we again recover our primal sense of wonder.

But, perhaps we have already lost our spontaneity and that subtle art of letting-things-be, of openness, of unwilling. Is the idea so foreign to us — becoming attuned again to the cycles of nature and to the internal sense or proprioceptivity of our own bodies, to the natural balance felt when we let go of control and learn again to act without intention? This is the meaning of the Chinese phrase *wu wei* — 'non-doing' or the lack of a controlling intentionality. In this light, *wu wei*, is not simply 'doing nothing' but rather acting without the intention to master or control the situation. It is suggestive of the spontaneity, the artlessness of nature herself. It simply means participating in nature, acting in concert with her movements.

This is our challenge. How to live a life of 'non-willing' or 'non-action' in a world so deeply committed to command and control? How does one even begin to assume such a posture? But then, perhaps these are just the ramblings of a madman, the idle thoughts of an old professor... quirky musings that do not apply to life in the real world? On the other hand, perhaps we should make an attempt to understand the Taoist view and the relevance of 'acting through non-action'.

First and foremost, *wei wu wei* implies a path of least resistance, a path that opens up when one stops pushing and allows nature to take its course; following where the way leads. It is a simple but not an easy path; nor is it readily accessible to a mind bent on planning and control. It is in large measure the result of serendipity, of remaining open to possibilities that present themselves. This is certainly a difficult challenge for us today, where everything from birth to death seems to demand more planning, control and the willful management of outcomes.

Perhaps the most pressing aspect to this challenge is the apparent irreversibility of clock-time and our stubborn awareness of time's forward march — an awareness that constitutes both our sense of self and our progress in life. Of course, our cultural toolkit — the skills we acquired during socialization — has focussed us exclusively on this unfolding and irreversible chronological trajectory, a temporal flow moving without rest from past to future with the expectation of achieving some desired outcome.

Yet there are rather clear indications that our most primitive ancestors (as far back as the early Pleistocene) had no sense of this linear-temporal progression. Rather, these primal forebears appear to have been immersed in a qualitatively different, rather unique experience of presence tied to the natural cycles of birth, death, return and renewal. For our earliest predecessors of the genus *Homo*, life was lived in the present — in closest proximity to the earth, engulfed in its uncultivated wildness, and absorbed in the periodic rhythms of nature's cycles. The earliest traces of cultural expression in cave-art, myth, and magic suggests this sense of presence, reaffirming an elemental kinship with the earth and the periodicity of return and renewal. They knew nothing of the so-called 'burden of history' that would later characterize modern consciousness.

The issues raised by the birth of historical consciousness — in other words, our unidirectional experience of time and the perception of life's meaning as somehow tied up with the movement from past to future — had always troubled me. It was especially unnerving since this view necessitated the unavoidable anticipation of my own death. To my thinking, this was contrary to how life should be lived. I should not live in fear and trembling over the realization that I too shall die. How depressing! Furthermore, this apprehension failed on many levels to acknowledge the spontaneity and periodicity of my lived-experience.

Yet, it was clear to me that civilization had already surrendered itself to an impersonal historical process that would not end well, but would culminate in personal and collective demise. Still, the question needed to be raised: Why should we be compelled to look forward with an ironic sense of resignation, existential dread, and the raw certainty of death? How unfulfilling! How frustrating! Could we not just as easily turn things around and learn to adopt a different perspective — no longer anticipating the 'end' but rather looking towards a new beginning? But this would not be looking back to the chronological past, instead it would be a way of 'looking' that discovers the potential for cyclical return and renewal. Certainly, this would entail a radically different type of perception, illuminating a qualitatively different temporal sense. Here we might uncover a new beginning, a moment at once grounding and renewing.

But what might be the source of such an experience? What type of perception might allow us to move beyond the conventional artifice of linear historical time? I

138

suspected that within each of us must reside some genetic memory-trace, a remnant of that primal openness and an inner sense of those natural cycles of return and renewal. Deep within our psyche, I thought, must reside a pre-conscious and primitive anamnesis lying beneath the surface of our otherwise conscious experience, a recollection embedded somewhat obscurely within our embodied existence. Yet, however we might characterize this experience, I imagine that such a memory-trace could provide us with the possibility of recovering a sense of presence that allows us to experience a more organic mode of dwelling. The meaning of one's life then would not be grasped by bravely or fearlessly moving headlong to death. Rather, life could be meaningfully constituted through an event of return and renewal. Such an event might itself be capable of exorcising the isolating and self-alienating demons of our historical consciousness. In fact, it might result in identification with an irreducibly full and present moment — to re-enchantment of the world in which we are always, already intimately engaged.

Let us consider briefly the following from Maurice Merleau-Ponty writing in *The Visible and the Invisible*.

> *We must reject the age-old assumption that places the body in the world and the seer in the body, or,*

conversely, the view that places the world and the body inside the seer as if in a box. Where are we to set the limit between the body and the world, since the world also is flesh? Where in the body are we to put the seer? By way of participation in and kinship with what is seen, our vision neither envelops the visible nor is enveloped by it… There is a reciprocal… intertwining of the one in the other. (p123)

Of course, this is a rather terse statement to unpack. But let me try to disclose its sense. I believe the philosopher is suggesting that here we come face to face with the natural co-inherence of the world-as-lived-by-the-body and so, with the primacy of perception. It is the natural intertwining of the lived-body-world that affords us the very possibility of sentient experience: of touching and being touched, of seeing and being seen, of hearing and being heard. Here is the basic intuition that I am at once subject and object concurrently, and that the world is both subject and object for me. As the philosopher asked, "Where are we to set the limit between the body and the world, since the world also is flesh?" In fact, it is in this very "reversibility" of subject and object in primitive thought that we recognize the underlying intuition behind the phenomenon of animism: that my flesh and the flesh of the world are one; my outline, the inline of

140

the territory; my totem an instantiation of the same power that animates the forest, the river, the sun, the moon, the stars and me. It is here that we might best grasp the concept of mythic participation. Like an umbilical cord joining us to mother-earth, the linkage of the lived-body-world is a thread that cannot be cut or broken.

In this light, it seems reasonable to suggest that our earliest hominid ancestors experienced an unbreakable bond between what we call 'self' and 'world.' This is diametrically opposed to how we feel that connection or, more correctly, the dis-connection today. For our ancient forebears the sense of 'self' or 'presence' was not as a discrete entity locked-up within a bag of skin facing an alien, external environment. Rather, they had a more autochthonous or indigenous sense of 'self' as an 'opening-on' and intertwining with the whole of nature, where life was felt ecstatically, an experience of 'being-outside-oneself' and participating the world directly. Owen Barfield, makes the following observation in *Saving The Appearances*.

> *[After the great transition to civilization, but prior to] the scientific revolution, [the individual still] did not feel himself isolated by his skin from the world outside to quite the same extent that we do*

[today]. He was integrated, or mortised into [the
world], each different part of himself being united
to a different part of it by some invisible thread...
(p.78)

The anthropologist, Lucien Levy-Bruhl appropriately
described this as "participation mystique" — a pre-
conscious co-inherence of the self in the other, and an
invisible but existential attachment to the surrounding
environment. This is the intuition at the heart of
animistic sensibility. It is a mode of being realized by a
visceral bodying-forth, whereby all elements, human and
non-human, touch, co-mingle, and inter-animate one
another in constituting a world. Here it becomes difficult
to talk about nature vs. culture or self vs. world; for the
two poles are simply reciprocal instantiations of one and
the same power, given various names by diverse
indigenous populations, including *mana* among the
Melanesians, *hasina* in Madagascar, *vaki* among the
Baltic Finns, *orendu* among the Iroquois Indians, or
wakanda among the Sioux. As Dōgen Zenji, 13th
Century founder of the Soto School of Zen put it:

I came to see clearly that mind is no other than
mountains and rivers and the great earth, the sun
and the moon and the stars.

So, if we reiterate Merleau-Ponty's earlier question —
'Where are we to put the limit between the body and the
world, since the world as well is flesh' — we find
ourselves unavoidably reflecting upon another idea of
his, the concept of '*chiasm*'. This is an image Merleau-
Ponty uses to make sense of that micro-gap or
divergence in the 'flesh' of the world that allows for a
crossing-over, overlapping or intertwining of body-as-
subject and the world-as-lived-by-the-body. As he
reminds us, it is in the very reversibility of flesh that this
chiasm shows itself.

> *[A] sort of dehiscence [or gap] opens my body in*
> *two, and because between my body looked-at and*
> *my body-looking, my body touched and my body*
> *touching, there is overlapping or encroachment, so*
> *that we may say that the things pass into us, as*
> *well as we into the things.*

Or again:

> *It is the thickness of flesh between the seer and the*
> *thing [seen that] is constitutive for the thing of its*
> *visibility as for the seer of his corporiety; it is not*
> *an obstacle between them, it is their means of*
> *communication.* (p. 135)

143

It is here that we crack open the doorway to the Eastern concept of *emptiness*; here mind and self are no longer seen as belonging to 'me' but rather to the flesh of the world in which 'I' participate through the flesh of my body-as-subject. Merleau-Ponty uses the concept of the flesh to evoke both separation and a crossing-over, giving voice to that emptiness (*Shunyata*) from whence arises the experience of intertwining, participation, and ecstasy — literally being-outside-oneself-participating-the-world.

In fact, 'emptiness' in this view is the simple realization that there is no separate "I" or "mine" — *shunyata* (*emptiness*) meaning that there is a lack of one's own-nature, that there is no independent 'self.' Considered a central text on Emptiness in the Mahayana Buddhist tradition, including Chan and Zen, *The Heart Sutra,* Verse 2 states:

Here, O Sariputra, bodily-form is emptiness; verily, emptiness is bodily-form. Apart from bodily-form there is no emptiness; so apart from emptiness there is no bodily-form. That which is emptiness is bodily-form; that which is bodily-form is emptiness. Likewise (the four aggregates) feeling, perception, mental imaging, and consciousness (all are devoid of substance).

These negations, of course, do not mean to suggest that sense experience and the flesh are nonexistent but, on the contrary, that they do not exist independently of a greater whole. As we read in Chapter Five of the *Tao Te Ching*:

> *Is not the space between Heaven and Earth like a bellows? It is empty, but lacks nothing.*

Remember, a central theme of the *Tao Te Ching* is the idea of *wei wu wei* or "action through non-action." In this context we may also recall Heidegger's concept of *gelassenheit* — 'repose,' 'waiting' or 'letting be.' It is in just such a posture that we allow *Being* to spring forth from Emptiness [空着]. I am suggesting, then, that Heidegger's sense of 'repose' or *gelassenheit* is closely allied with the practice of emptiness in both Chan and Zen Buddhist traditions. As Heidegger himself queries us regarding meditative thinking: "Does man still dwell calmly between heaven and earth?" (*Gelassenheit*, p. 48)

This imagery — dwelling between heaven and earth — forces us yet again to acknowledge the apparent emptiness of being located in neither realm, but rather existing within that space, that *chaism* or inter-twining; and thereby, our remaining open to the mystery of existence. For Heidegger this is a unique way of being.

As he summarizes: "We are to do nothing but wait." [*Wir sollen nichts tun sondern warten*] (*Gelassenheit*, p. 35.) This is how one remains open to mystery, to possibility. And here we come to Heidegger's idea of "waking up"— a mode of enlightenment attributable to the kind of meditative thinking that waits. He reminds us in *The Question Concerning Technology*: Be "the one who waits, the one who attends upon the coming into presence of Being..." (p. 41)

Deconstructing Politics Today

As Ron DeSantis prepares his bid for a 2024 presidential run, he's apparently committed to a strategy reminiscent of the 'Woke Left' he so brutally criticizes. I'm referring of course to the Florida Governor's focus on removing, eliminating, or perhaps 'cancelling' specific elements of our common cultural history, dismissing the legacy of black slavery, and throwing down a gauntlet before liberal-minded educators. Despite vociferous disagreement from various quarters concerning his recent policies outlawing certain types of literature in Florida's elementary and secondary schools, DeSantis has now set his sights on regulating which view of history (including black history) the state universities in Florida may offer students as well. His position seems just as blind to key elements of our well-storied history as is that of the 'Woke Left' — each side seeking to 'cancel' specific elements of our past whether in literature, history, or artifacts found to be objectionable.

1.

In 2021 we witnessed emergence of something
called the Reawaken America Tour, a not unlikely
assembly of misfits and madmen led by disgraced
United States General Michael Flynn in league with
Oklahoma conspiracy theorist and movement
founder, Clay Clark. With Eric Trump in tow, this
group emerged as just one more gathering of far-
right extremists and Christian nationalists who
believed they were walking with Jesus along the
road to Golgotha giving voice to a proselytizing
theology that has thrust itself into the center of
American politics; it was just another fine example
of re-mythologizing taking center stage in this
bewildering cultural debate. Some have even
suggested that this nationalistic ideology has
become a key feature of current evangelical belief,
suggesting that this may be the strangest expression
of faith since the prophets of Baal "shouted louder,
and gashed themselves with knives and spears . . .
until the blood streamed over them." (1)

Much like a plurality of the 'Woke' crowd he
vehemently criticizes, Governor DeSantis seems
increasingly uncomfortable with specific aspects of
our cultural past that he dismisses as not simply

unworthy of study, but positively harmful. He is ready to discard elements within our collective American memory that he judges antithetical to his myopic views and confused values — creating a veritable clutch on both thought and speech within and outside of the Sunshine State. But what is the net effect of this attack on our cultural history? And what happens if his machinations succeed nationally in erasing even select elements of tradition that have been found problematic by his questionable judgement? That would be quite a slippery slope indeed.

2.

Let's shift gears here momentarily to consider the philosophical issue of 'historicity' — that is to say, our being situated within a specific cultural milieu and historical tradition. Our concrete placement within the temporal flow of history provides us with our principal 'horizon of understanding'; in short, it gives us the ability to grasp anything whatsoever. Simply stated, we are always, already there — within the flow of history — and that presence remains foundational for our understanding of what is past. In his work, *Truth and Method*, Hans-Georg Gadamer states this succinctly:

Our attempts to understand... depend upon the
questions which our own cultural environment
allows us to raise... Our present perspective
always involves a relationship to the past... (2)

As the philosopher here suggests, there is a horizon
— inclusive of both past and present — against
which all understanding naturally occurs. This
provides the ground or backdrop by means of which
we are able grasp the sense of any specific text,
artifact, communication, or situation. Gadamer calls
this capacity 'pre-understanding.' As he contends,
all acts of understanding are guided in advance by
certain presuppositions that we already hold. In
short, there is no truly objective perspective.
Understanding always depends upon and emerges
from that which we have previously understood,
that is to say, from presuppositions already lodged
and at work within us. Even the simple act of
choosing a topic for investigation is grounded in
some pre-conscious grasp of the subject matter at
hand — guided in advance by specific attitudes or
ways of looking at the world. In short, we single out
or choose items for consideration based upon
preliminary predispositions or 'prejudices'.

Furthermore, our ability to understand the past, or even one another, is influenced by how we *always, already* find ourselves situated within our cultural horizon with its unique historical trajectory. This holds true for the individual, the group, as well as the culture as a whole. And as 'pre-understanding' provides the ground, genuine understanding always occurs by means of a "fusion of horizons" — of the past with the present, of the alien with the familiar, of my view with that of the Other. It is in such a fusion that the event of understanding ultimately rests. We are historical creatures, not because we have a history, but the reverse. We have and share a history because we are fundamentally historical through and through.

Finally, the very possibility of having a horizon is due to those aforementioned prejudices that help shape what we hear, read or otherwise understand. This is the case whether we are considering a dialogue among friends, a homily at church, a passage from Dostoyevsky, a news clip from across the world, or an aberrant tweet out of Mar-a-Lago. Shakespeare had it right when he wrote: "What is past is prologue". (3) In short, the past is foundational for understanding anything whatsoever. Certain predispositions *always, already* influence the way in which we read, hear, or otherwise understand a communication. In this event, any attempt to *cancel* or erase part of the tradition — texts, histories, artifacts, persons — not only destroys cultural memory, it concurrently eats away at the ground upon which a common understanding is made possible in the first place. The result of such 'cancelling' is that our complex, multi-dimensional culture is transformed into a flat-screen upon which only the latest revisionary spectacle is available. The remainder is lost in a fiery conflagration of burning books, icons, and other disparate images.

3.

Our capacity for understanding is thus historical at its core. The very language in which we converse has a legacy and a tradition that can neither be forgotten nor ignored. "The past is never dead," wrote William Faulkner; "It is not even past."(4) But if we let that happen, indeed if we allow the past to be erased, if we bend to censorship — from either the Left or the Right — we risk allowing key elements of our past to die in this very act of erasure. In this event, the sense of an unfolding historical narrative that helped define our lives will be distorted, short-circuiting our capacity for understanding anything whatsoever. In brief, we may find ourselves rudderless and without a grounding narrative arc. If we insist, in other words, on erasing specific elements of our cultural tradition, parts of our past — breaking or disrupting the circle of understanding that helps ground us — we only succeed in destroying our power to grasp who we are and whence we came. In this event, our ability to interpret current events will be short-circuited, cut off from that which has given rise to our present and whatever it is that we know. It is more than disingenuous, indeed it is dangerous, if we "aspire to wash away a complicated past and replace it with one that is beyond rebuke." (5)

Are there imperfections embedded within the great variety of our literary and cultural history? Of course there are! Dr. Seuss or even Mark Twain, for example, were writing at a different time, under the influence of different social norms and sensitivities. But every text necessarily retains the weight and influence of its own concrete placement within the tradition, its own unique history of understanding between its covers. Yet so-called 'flaws' in a work of art or a text are not reason enough for making "the works of important artists disappear…" (6)

Eliminating or silencing such works is not simply censorship. It represents a refusal to acknowledge and a failure to engage the self-understanding of the artist and the culture that gave rise to the work in the first place; it betrays our inability to grasp its relevance or bring the work meaningfully into the present, thereby inhibiting expansion of our own horizon of understanding. In fact, it is best when trying to understand the Other — be it a text, work of art, or another person — that we positively engage in a dialogue to expand our horizon of understanding, not only of the past but of our present situation as well. This helps move us forward, enhancing self-understanding while enabling us to grasp the Other in a continuously expanding circle. It is an ongoing game in which our 'being-with-others' always, already naturally occurs. As Gadamer maintains:

> *In speaking with each other we constantly pass over into the thought world of the other; we engage him, and he engages us. So we adapt ourselves to each other in a preliminary way until the game of giving and taking — real dialogue — begins.* (7)

Gadamer concludes that such a dialogue will always lead to an enrichment of the self, never to its loss or diminution. And these observations hold true for dealing with the written word as well:

> *To understand a text is to come to understand oneself in dialogue. A text yields understanding only when what is said in the text begins to find expression in [one's] own language...* (8)

But if we try to silence the text, if we demand the erasure or cancelling of its statement, we thereby deny ourselves an opportunity to understand our history and ourselves more fully; we lose that capacity to enlarge our horizon of understanding. In short, we lose the possibility for that unique dialogue wherein something new may come into being.

The challenges of cancelling tradition and history are obviously problematic to say the least; we may erase the memory of the Klu Klux Klan, for example, but we do so at our own peril. Indeed, the re-emergence of far-right anti-government white nationalist movements — including the Boogaloo Boys, Proud Boys, Three-Percenters, and QAnon —

now exercising influence over a not insubstantial block of the American electorate indicate just how forcefully our past can come roaring back to dictate the future trajectory of culture. And while real history is not always to be endorsed or emulated, it certainly needs to be taken account of, if for no other reason than allowing us to reckon with that tradition as we adjudicate the norms of current and evolving social praxis. In short, the past is never gone but always with us whether or not it we allow it to enlighten or guide us; it is, and will always remain, prologue.

We return now ever so briefly to Mr. DeSantis. His disregard or denial of history is reflected in various legislative maneuvers intended to cancel portions of our cultural legacy and those who would proffer a worldview contradicting his politically charged understanding. As one commentator has suggested,

> *From banning books to dictating curricula, Republicans are the real cancelers... [Indeed], the right is far more guilty than the left of the crime of cancel culture.* (9)

And it appears that Ron DeSantis is the Republican Canceler in Chief.

Notes

1) *Old Testament*, 1Kings, 18:28-29

2) Hans Georg-Gadamer, *Philosophical Hermeneutics*, 56

3) William Shakespeare, *The Tempest*

4) William Faulkner, *Requiem for a Nun*

5) B. Wallace, "Who is In Charge of Cancel Culture," *New Yorker*, Mar 11, 2021

6) Elisha Fieldstadt, NBC News, Mar 9, 2021

7) Hans-Georg Gadamer, *Philosophical Hermeneutics*, 57

8) Ibid

9) "Altercation: There Is a Cancel Culture, and It's the Right That's Advancing It," Eric Alterman, The American Prospect, April 15, 2022

Hypotaxis, Hierarchy, and Happiness
On the Politics of Linguistic Recursion

*As the written word began speaking,
the stones fell silent... the trees became mute, the other
animals dumb.* (1)

Among linguistic theoreticians, Noam Chomsky is a seminal figure. Among his contributions, Chomsky has argued that humankind has an inborn "universal generative grammar" — a natural capacity allowing for the possibility of language acquisition. One of the unique characteristics of this generative grammar is what he calls "recursion." This is a process of "embedding" or "nesting" smaller phrases within larger linguistic units — what may be called semantic, syntactic, and logistic subordination.

Chomsky claims that this process of subordination or *recursion* is what enables the construction of more complex or "hypotactic" language units: for example, "I went to the store because I needed to buy some milk." With hypotaxis, clauses in a sentence or paragraph are subordinated to one another, focusing attention on what is of more importance within the larger linguistic unit.

Parataxis, on the other hand, works without subordinating conjunctions or clauses. A clear example of parataxis would be Julius Caesar's famous words: "I came, I saw, I conquered." Or we might say, referring to our example above: "I went to the store. I needed to buy some milk." Parataxis thus refers to language in which each phrase or clause in a larger grammatical unit carries equal weighting, none of the clauses subordinated one to another in a hierarchical scheme. By means of subordination, then, recursion allows for the possibility of hierarchization in the linguistic and, as I will argue, in the political realm as well.

We now raise the following question: Is recursion, that is to say, linguistic subordination, essential to all human language, or is it only a property of some language families, some forms of language usage? For example, is there any relationship between linguistic recursion and literacy; between 'hypotactic' subordination in language and the emergence of socio-political hierarchies? Further to the point, is the hierarchical ordering and syntactic subordination we find in the written text either a 'model of' or a 'model for' the subordination we find on the battlefield, in a corporate boardroom, within a government bureaucracy, or in the theatre of political debate? Everything about today's dominant global culture reeks of hierarchy and subordination, whether in democratic dress or military uniform. As Chomsky himself has admitted, no government is truly representative; each has its "own power, serving segments of the population that are dominant and rich," that is to say, at the top of the socio-economic power hierarchy. (2)

In short, is it possible that social, economic, and political hierarchies are connected in some way to the recursive linguistic hierarchies embedded within our written tongues? And was there some prior condition, before the birth of literacy (the written word) perhaps, where linguistic recursion and hierarchy did not yet exist, or at least did not dominate the field of human cognition and communication?

In the past several years, Daniel Everett, Dean of Arts and Sciences at Bentley University in Massachusetts, and former Chair of the Department of Languages, Literatures and Cultures at Illinois State University, published a groundbreaking work on the remote Piraha tribe, a group of hunter-gatherers living on the edge of the rain forest along the Maici River in Brazil's Amazon region.(3) For thirty years Everett lived with this tribe studying their language and culture. The Piraha's unwritten tongue (spoken, sung and hummed) consists of just eight consonants and three vowels, and lacks many of the grammatical characteristics found in other languages. Especially noteworthy, it lacks the phenomenon of recursion (linguistic subordination) that Chomsky claimed was central to all human languages. As Everett said in a 2012 interview:

All languages have unique characteristics, but Pirahã just seems to have so many unique characteristics. Things that we didn't expect. I mean the absence of numbers, the absence of counting and colours, the absence of creation myths, and the refusal to talk about the distant past or the distant future. A number of things like this, including, the special characteristic of recursion, the ability to keep a process going in the syntax forever. (4)

And this, he believes, says something about what is important in the Piraha culture. As Everett depicts their worldview, the locus of concern and attention is on . . .

*[t]he immediacy of experience, not to worry
about the future or past, and not talk about
what you have not seen or heard. They hunt,
fish and share their food; the rest of the time
they laugh, talk, spend time enjoying
themselves... What struck me was their lack of
superstition, their contentment with life as they
found it. And their happiness! I have never
seen people facing so many difficulties, with so
much grace: it deeply impressed me.* (5)

Perhaps this is where we find a turning point in
human history, what social anthropologist Jack
Goody called "the domestication of the savage
mind," (6) or the birth of literacy. It is here, I wager,
that we find the ascendancy of linguistic hierarchy
and 'hypotactic' space-time over 'paratactic'
presence, the future over the present, law over
custom, and history over myth. I would like to
spend just a few minutes on the differences in
perception and worldview.

As cultural historian Marvin Bram contends in *The
Recovery Of The West*, "Parataxis suggests
coordination more than subordination, and any
number of sequences rather than a single correct
sequence." In short, parataxis de-hierarchizes. The

flatter, coordinate, non-orderliness of a paratactic worldview seems rather primitive or prosaic to someone operating within the more civilized, tightly structured, hypotactic logistic. Bram continues:

> *Parataxis is concerned with the concrete thing itself, the local and contained, and the moment, rather than with relationships among abstract things and over-arching spatial and temporal schemes... Parataxis space and time make dramatic antitheses to their hypotactic counterparts.* (7)

For example, someone walking down a forest path seeing 'paratactically' will observe much more than a person looking 'hypotactically' along the same path but seeing only what is of interest to him; hypotactical vision is hierarchizing. Paratactic visual space on the other hand will be fuller, pregnant with signification. As Bram concludes,

> *This phenomenon of paratactic persons taking in more of the world, living in a fuller world than hypotactic persons, has been reported time and time again by (hypotactic) travelers among (paratactic) traditional peoples.* (8)

It is interesting to note in this regard how the orderly rows of plowed fields led to urban surpluses. These in turn were accounted for through enumeration of linear tables of numbers in the written records of our earliest kingdoms and nation states — the first signs of writing, along with documented codes of social control. The more haphazard plots of early Neolithic horticulturalists were simply not comparable with the tilled and plowed fields of the agriculturalist, just as the meandering herds of sheep among the earliest shepherds cannot compare to the meticulously aligned metal stalls of the modern abattoir. And the language of control, the written document, was key to building the assorted hierarchies that would henceforth manage the herds, the fields, the supplies, and the citizens, as well as the outsiders. Legal institutions, advocates and judges, guilt and innocence, along with police forces and the military were born in that self-same moment of our earliest history. It is here that the trajectory of the West was born.

Even in the language of Genesis, the story of Babel is not just about the multiplicity of tongues as I already suggested in an earlier post. It is rather a depiction of the overarching structural integrity of a burgeoning universal linguistic, and its ability to subordinate and unify disparate members of the citizenry within a shared grammar and worldview. I would say this story is a mythological recognition of the trajectory of the written word — its capacity for disambiguation and hierarchization, thus enabling greater displays of command and control.

The building of cities, the concrete establishment of civilization — the Tower of Babel — was dependent upon the unambiguous nature of the written word, and the hierarchical control it afforded the literati of the imperial court. No doubt, much was gained with the move to literacy, with the ascendance of univocality, the written record of history, the significance of the past and the value of the future. It also provided the mechanism for bureaucratic structures and laws to manage the new menagerie of human community, and realize the possibilities that civilized life now afforded. Yet, there was also born regret for a past poorly lived and anxiety over a future still uncertain, in short, the weighty terror of historical consciousness, and the realization that I too will die someday. As Bram reminds us,

*In paratactic time there is little past because
there are no complete logistic structures to be
sought there, and there is little future because
there is no need for a place in which to
complete incomplete logistic structures. There
is certainly a present, gathering to itself much
of the energy that hypotactic persons give to
the past and future, and inhabited by full
persons and full objects: a full present. The
present of hypotactic time often enough takes
third place behind the past and the future,
depleted of energy: an empty present.* (9)

But, what exactly was lost in this transformation to
a 'hypotactic' word — in the subordination of
thought and speech within the universal grammar of
literacy, univocality, and finally, the sterile logic of
the syllogism and mathematics?

The cognitive changes produced resounding
reverberations for all generations to follow,
entrenched, as humanity would become, in new
organizational hierarchies that appeared — the
formal institutions of civil society. Was it not
literacy, giving prominence to a 'hierarchizing'
logistic, that provided momentum to both the
political and scientific objectification of nature and

human relations? An incipient temperament for this new logistic, and a newly constructed worldview, affected every dimension of life as civilization spread, and cities continued to populate the globe over subsequent millennia. Following language development, it was the objectification of nature — destroying the power and thickness of a pre-objective present — that led ineluctably to a de-animation of nature and the subsequent theoretical construction of transcendent powers — gods, goddesses, the noumena, or eventually, the abstract laws of modern physics.

Hypotaxis and hierarchy, mathematics and the syllogism, in short, literacy has allowed us to slice and dice the world, dissecting it in so many ways. Perhaps it is time to bandage those cuts and let the healing begin, if it is not already too late. In hindsight, perhaps we might all be better off had we never been taught to read or write, or paint by numbers in the first place — like the Piraha. Perhaps the globe wouldn't be quite the mess it is today had it only been otherwise. Perhaps, as growing evidence from psychoanalytic practice suggests, if we could once again experience rich 'paratactic' wholes we might in fact become happier people — like the Piraha!

Notes

(1) Abram, David, *The Spell of the Sensuous*, 1996,
    p. 131.

(2) Chomsky, Noam, Interview with Michael
Wilson, *Modern Success*

(3) Everett, Daniel, *Don't Sleep, There Are Snakes*,
Pantheon (2008)

(4) Everett, Daniel, Interview by Robert McCrum,
The Observer, 25 March 2012

(5) Godrèche, Dominique, "The Amazon's Pirahã
People's Secret to Happiness", 25 June, 2012

(6) Goody, Jack, *The Domestication of the Savage
Mind*, Oxford

(7) Bram, Marvin, *The Recovery of The West*, 2002,
Exlibris, pp. 25-26

(8) Bram, Ibid

(9) Bram, Ibid

The Corporate State

State is the name of the coldest of all cold monsters.
Coldly it tells lies too; and this lie crawls out of its
mouth: 'I, the state, am the people.' That is a lie!
(Nietzsche, *Thus Spake Zarathustra*)

There's quite a lot of talk today about the State and
specifically the Corporate State. This is particularly
alarming in light of the political issues with which
we are now grappling. Critiquing this 'legal fiction,'
renowned war correspondent and journalist, Chris
Hedges, asks: "When did the dead hand of the
corporate state become unassailable?"

While the murky beginnings of human community
were characterized by primal bonds of kinship, it is
rather difficult to account for the cold calculating
systems of hierarchy within which our daily lives
have managed to become entrenched. Over the past
several millennia, we have moved from kinship,
through kingship, and finally to the modern State.
Whether we consider the marketing juggernaut of
the West, the theocratic Middle-East, or Communist
regimes in China and Cuba — elements of control,
corruption, and condescension seem to run rampant

everywhere we find the State. Similar scenarios repeat themselves, more or less, in one international venue after another. The State appears in each case as a source of conflict demanding resolution.

The State — what exactly is this entity? Of utmost significance for our present inquiry, the State may be understood as the chief mechanism behind the break-down of our original bonds of kinship (Plato), only to be replaced with new bonds of citizenship. As Marvin Bram has observed:

> *The first emergence of civilization in the Middle East, and all subsequent civilized nations, were constructed on the break-up of their pre-urban clans. (Recovery of the West, 26)*

As Rousseau has suggested — the principal function of the State is destruction of the natural man in order to reconstitute him or her with a new nature. In *The Social Contract* he writes:

> *[The Legislator] must, in a word, take man's own forces away from him in order to give him forces which are foreign to him and which he cannot use without the help of*

others. The more the natural forces are
dead and annihilated the greater and more
lasting the acquired ones... [II, 7]

In short, the reconstitution of the individual person
in the image of a loyal and dependent citizen-
subject is a principal concern of the State.

Second, the State itself is an entity given life by
some form of social contract or arrangement (either
implied or explicit). Under the best circumstances,
such agreement might result in production of an
actual document, perhaps one composed by the
would-be legislators themselves. Witness the white-
wigged, aristocratic gentlemen-attorneys at the
Constitutional Convention who founded the
American Republic and produced its cherished
social contract.

Third, the State maintains a monopoly on the use of
physical force — police, detention, and military
power — to create public order while expanding its
own authority and regime beyond its borders. As
principal executive over the body-politic, the State
alone has license to exercise force in achieving
compliance with its demands, domestically or
internationally. In this respect, it thrives on a

171

condition of "permanent war and fear" leading to ongoing "conquest abroad and repression at home." (Chris Hedges, *TruthDig*)

And what precisely is the body politic? While Rousseau and others have referred to the Sovereign or autocratic ruler as the body-politic, it is more appropriate in our current discussion to understand the term as referring to the governed, the citizen-body of the State, the electorate, if you will. Indeed, in key respects the nation itself has often been regarded as a "corporate entity" — a *corps* or body — analogous in many respects to a human body, with the State Sovereign or Legislator as its head. It is the body (*corpus*) of citizenry comprising the State – "*le corps-etat*." These citizens — persons legally subject to the controlling authority of the State — are parts of the body, obliged to perform according to its rule of law.

Moreover, as citizen-subjects these persons are educated according to State curricula, insuring ideological conformity and harmonious performance as integrated members within the complex web of politically sanctioned institutional relations. Accordingly, the citizen-subjects serve inadvertently to maintain the State, its legislative authority, as well as their own conditional bondage to the institutional, legal, and executive powers of the head. But, as some scholars have noted, we must never confuse the civil rule of law with that primal authority of kinship-based custom. As Stanley Diamond contends:

> *[L]aw is symptomatic of the emergence of the State... and cannot be defined as the simple passage of custom into law. Passage to the legal order represents a transition from the primitive kinship-based community to the class-structured polity.* (Stanley Diamond, *In Search Of The Primitive: A Critique Of Civilization,* 255 -260)

Quoting Paul Radin, Diamond concludes:

> *[C]ustoms are an integral part of the life of primitive peoples. There is no compulsive submission to them."* (256)

This is a fundamental differentiator between the inherited values of a kinship-based egalitarian clan and those of the civilized State with their enforced imposition and legally binding demands upon a 'corporate' body. And what about the modern corporation? The word "corporation" also derives from the Latin *corps* (body); it too is a legal fiction, representing a 'body' of persons authorized to act collectively as an individual vis-a-vis the State. This legal fiction embodies (*corporare*) and, hence, serves to protect those persons or actors hidden beneath the cloak of its *corporatio*, while providing them leeway within the world of the unincorporated masses. The modern corporation, then, is nothing more than an avatar, an apparent manifestation or incarnation of powers lurking behind the corporate veil and its logo, the visible symbol of the corpus or corporate body.

I would suggest, however, that the modern corporation, in its basic structure and functionality, was prefigured in the origins of the State in relation to the body-politic. The grades of personnel on a corporate organization chart are reflective of classes of citizens, and the degree of personal alienation among its employees are reflected in the degree of specialization. The embracing of hierarchy, the status-based and largely top-down organizational structure, the focus on clear institutionalization of corporate culture, the inculcation of personnel to the rules of corporate policy and procedure, the flow of 'corporate politics,' the re-socialization and full integration of employees as members of the corporate team (*corps-etat*); these are all elements derived originally from the State. It is no wonder, then, that the State should now be seen as a corporate entity, in fact, the Corporate State may be the final flowering of its very nature, perhaps signaling the end of history itself, as Francis Fukuyama clearly celebrated in his book of that title. Indeed, power and the accumulation of wealth have always been twin hallmarks of civilized political hierarchy. It stands to reason that the eleventh-hour union of politics and capital in the creation of modern *corporatocracy* would take place, so that now the world's most powerful State military would be clearly and unambiguously under the control of corporate money, doing the bidding of their commercial interests.

Furthermore, it is not so strange to consider corporations as artificial persons. After all, as individual citizens of the State, we too are artificial persons — subjects — created by diverse impersonal institutional relations. The real difference between "natural" citizens and "corporate" citizens is that the persons hiding within the corporate body have extraordinary protections from normal judicial and legal sanctions, just as do those who occupy our State Houses and our Federal hierarchies. Us unincorporated members of the body politic are not so advantaged.

Finally, in some respects, there may be a traceable but much diluted resemblance between our uncritical allegiances to the modern corporation, the body-politic, or the State, and those more intimate relations obtaining between archaic humanity, their totems and clans. We tend to identify in some manner with corporate sponsors, employers, nation-states, or our favorite football teams, although perhaps not as comfortably as our progenitors once identified with their tribes, bands, and totem animals. Maybe these civilized associations are too abstract and, therefore, somewhat hollow replacements for the participatory relations that once held us comfortably and customarily within a kinship group of real consanguine and egalitarian relations. In any event, such associations seem to survive as remnants of much more primitive conditions, providing strange comfort in our current political storms.

Burning Down the House

How do we make sense of the frightening contours emerging within America's political landscape, specifically those menacing views on the Right? This question requires attention to the two men currently 'bookending' the Republican presidential race. Of course, we've already seen full-throated authoritarian behaviors from both 'the Donald' and 'Ronald,' the twin front-runners for their party's upcoming nomination. But, now we need to take a deeper dive into the specific inanity and insanity that each represents.

We all had front row seats, and in living color no less, to Trump's multifaceted efforts at overturning Joe Biden's election victory — even directing an armed mob to overrun the Capital in a desperate attempt to claw-back his hold on the seat of power. DeSantis, on the other hand, has been engaged in his own treacherous political machinations — implementing a multi-pronged assault on the more progressive currents in American culture. Indeed, he seems intent on curtailing, if not eliminating, our basic freedoms of speech, choice, and association. If either of these two men wins the presidency, he will be intent on 'burning down the house'. For no other reason, the current situation requires serious consideration concerning the nature and role of civil government and where our politics stand now.

As argued earlier, in ancient Greece the spadework was already laid and battle-lines drawn so philosophers could make the ultimate cut, separating 'nature' from 'culture'. Thereafter Plato hypothesized the existence of a hierarchically organized human soul, where the rational element (well trained by culture and convention) ruled over the lower, concupiscent part — our baser and insatiable animal desires. In short, hypotheses were already floated to justify the model of hierarchical civil society, including its dominion over, and management of the body-politic.

Throughout the ancient world, into medieval times, and right up to the present, civil society was thus viewed as a necessary and coercive corrective to the inherent egoism and selfishness of human nature — mankind's allegedly brutish instincts. While Freud made this the cornerstone of his early twentieth century work, *The Future of an Illusion*, Marshall Sahlins confirmed in *The Western Illusion of Human Nature* that the concept of "Original Sin pretty

178

much sealed the deal in Christendom for centuries to come." Or, as Elaine Pagels argued in *Adam, Eve, and the Serpent*:

> *St. Augustine . . . offered an analysis of human nature that became, for better and for worse, the heritage of all subsequent generations of Western Christians and a major influence on their psychological and political thinking.*

Thus, already among pre-Socratic philosophers and early Church Fathers lay the theoretical groundwork for political philosophers in the West, including Enlightenment thinkers like Thomas Hobbes and Jean-Jacques Rousseau — themselves relying upon concepts already in the air from the time of Thucydides. In his classic work, *The Social Contract*, Rousseau argues that the principal function of civil government is sublimation of the natural man in order to recreate him with a 'moral' coat of armor. As he summarized:

> *[The legislator must] feel himself capable, so to speak, of changing human nature, transforming each individual, who is by himself a complete and solitary whole, into*

part of a greater whole from which that
individual as it were gets his life and his
being; weaken man's constitution to strengthen
it; substitute a partial and moral existence for
the physical and independent existence which
we all have received from nature.

But, it may behoove us at this point to recall Dmitri
Razumikhin's words in Dostoyevsky's novel, *Crime
and Punishment*: "To go wrong in one's own way is
better than to go right in someone else's." And that
raises a central issue for our current discussion.
Where do the responsibilities of the State end, and
the rights of the individual begin? This question
haunts our present democratic republic as we
struggle with the specter of authoritarianism
emanating not only from State Houses across this
land, but from the White House as well if either of
those two Republican candidates (Ronald or
Donald) proves successful in his bid for the
presidency.

More concretely: how should we understand
DeSantis' endless attacks on self-determination and
individual choice? In fact, the man's philosophy
appears to require precisely the sort of 'substitution'
that Rousseau warns us about in the above quote.

Nor should we ignore the other autocrat in the room, Donald Trump, whose Caligula-like aspirations are more than evident in word and deed.

But now the question must be posed: Why does civil society require, indeed compel, complete acquiescence and obedience to its norms — to a 'moral' existence on its own terms? Perhaps Dostoyevsky was correct. Is it not better to falter while pursuing one's own direction, than simply acquiescing — becoming a carbon copy of your neighbor? Do we really need either of these authoritarians (the Donald or Ronald) working to curtail or restrict those individual rights we have been given by nature?

The fact of the matter is, led by the likes of these two candidates, the Republicans seem to be burning down their own house! Perhaps, then, we need only stand back and watch the conflagration as Chris Christie explodes across our TV screens and takes the fight straight to the boys.

The Shaman in Trump's Cargo Cult

What I found most fascinating about the attack and attempted coup on our Capitol in January of 2021 was the presence of America's very own shaman all tricked-out in buffalo-horns and a tattooed midriff. Let's begin by exploring not only the nature and function of this self-described shaman, but also the significance of QAnon as a uniquely American cargo cult, and the role of their apparent savior in the events that transpired.

In his classic study of cargo cults, *The Trumpet Shall Sound*, British sociologist Peter Worsley provides an overview of this uniquely Melanesian phenomenon.

> *[In these] strange religious movements ... a prophet announces the imminence of the end of the world in a cataclysm which will destroy everything. Then the ancestors will return, or God, or some other liberating power, will appear, bringing all the goods the people desire, and ushering in a reign of eternal bliss.* (1)

While ethnographers have noted that the term 'cargo' originally referred to highly sought-after Western goods, they acknowledge that it also signaled the "expectation of moral salvation, existential respect, and the proto-nationalistic desire for political autonomy."(2) The term cargo-cult thus appears as exemplary of any social movement aspiring to renewed religious and political significance.

Worsley correctly identifies these cults as specifically millenarian movements bent on prosecuting an agenda of social unrest and political change. Preparing for a salvific event, these cults actively anticipate an apocalyptic conclusion of the old world and dramatic arrival of a new order. It appears, then, that QAnon followers together with their self-styled shaman were fiercely, if not brutally, advancing just such an event of deliverance courtesy of their would-be savior, Donald Trump.

The millenarian aspects of the Trump campaign — the magical nativism and promise of a world restored — have received surprisingly little comment although together with his erratic ravings they were perhaps its most striking features. (3)

QAnon certainly appears in key points as a modern-day cargo cult, harboring belief in the imminence of a transformative eschatological event. It is this kind of grandiose and ostensibly magical thinking that underlay the attack on our Capitol; it was an event whose teleological intention was clearly telegraphed — the hope of ushering in a new age with their 'cargo prophet' Trump restored to his rightful thrown. As deranged as this scenario may sound, describing it with such archetypal imagery here is not in the least bit gratuitous.

In point of fact, the nativistic and purportedly spiritual constitution of this modern day cult raises important questions regarding the nature of its proto-religious origin. To this end, we should consider the specific role played by their self-styled shaman in advancing the cult's activity. Attempting to grasp the character of the shaman, let's begin by considering shamanism in its more pristine form within archaic and more traditional cultures.

Typically found among hunter-gatherer, pastoral, or simple agricultural societies, the shaman's role in such communities was continuous with older forms of magico-religious practice dating back perhaps as early as the late Paleolithic. Since the beginning of

184

the 20th century, ethnologists and anthropologists have used the terms shaman, medicine-man, sorcerer, witch-doctor, and magician somewhat interchangeably, denoting individuals who possess special healing and other sacred powers found in nearly all traditional cultures. Furthermore, the term 'shaman' has been used to describe like phenomena among civilized peoples as well. For example, we find discussions of Indian, Iranian, German, Chinese, even Babylonian shamanism. And in the USA today, shamanism itself has apparently become the latest New Age phenomenon, replacing Buddhism as the hot religious practice of the 21st century.

As one can well imagine, shamanism is a rather tricky term to pin down because it has been used in diverse socio-cultural contexts. Such conceptual complexity often serves to confuse understanding of the phenomenon itself. At its core, we can say that shamanism refers to a magico-religious complex already in evidence among Neolithic societies and indigenous cultures. And, while there have been shamans leading groups into battle — for example, among the Buryat tribes resisting Russian colonization in the 17th and 18th centuries — the shaman's role is traditionally that of healer, spiritual guide, and medicine man; his objective is to maintain the health of the tribe and conduct souls of the dead safely into the afterlife.

As well, there are examples of traditional and indigenous peoples pushing back against the modern bastardization of their sacred traditions. As recently as 1993 during an international summit of US and Canadian Lakota, Dakota and Nakota peoples, about 500 representatives from forty different indigenous tribes unanimously passed a declaration to oppose exploitation of their spiritual roots. As one resolution plainly stated:

> *We assert a posture of zero-tolerance for any 'white man's shaman' who rises from within our own communities to 'authorize' the expropriation of our ceremonial ways by non-Indians; all such 'plastic medicine men' are enemies of the Lakota, Dakota and Nakota people.* (4)

While in traditional cultures the shaman functions as healer, prophet, and custodian of the sacred — working to insure maintenance of cultural harmony and tribal continuity — apparently our

QAnon shaman did not understand his role. Instead of promoting healing, he rather sought to inflict pain and division, determined to overturn the social order destroying our cultural and political framework.

So when this Navy veteran, Jacob Chansley, self-described shaman, rose up to lead a violent gang of insurrectionists into the Capitol, he was neither a 'metaphysical warrior' nor the 'compassionate healer' as he proclaimed to be in Facebook. A self-described 'con-spiritualist' (something at the intersection of conspiracy theorist and New Age mystic), he was convinced that destruction of the old order was necessary to bring about a resurrected Trump and a new world order, not unlike the Ascension of Christ or a Great Awakening. This self-styled crank was even prepared to capture and/or assassinate elected government officials in order to actualize the hoped-for apocalyptic event. Indeed, many QAnon believers held tight to their faith that a battle should ensue between the forces of good and powers of darkness. In large measure, that was their mission and desired outcome.

[A] biblical rapture of sorts or 'storm' would rain down on the country during the

inauguration at noon on Wednesday — when forces amassed by Trump would appear to arrest Biden and other Democrats on live TV while Trump would be sworn in for a second term. (5)

Channeling much of this biblical and apocalyptic language, candidate-Trump continued promulgating such a proleptic vision, forewarning us of a "final battle" still to come, while threatening "death and destruction" if he would be charged with any crime. Much of his rhetoric was eschatological and fiercely apocalyptic — foreshadowing an end time, including destruction of the infidels, and his own ascension back onto a thrown of glory.

And so, a collection of largely white men emboldened by the Proud and the Boogaloo Boys, became unwitting foot-soldiers in defense of an incarnation of Mephistopheles. And just like an estranged prophet wandering the wilderness, this shaman obediently played his part as Fool leading insurrectionists to the Capitol. There they would seek-out enemies of their king, attempt to destroy his adversaries, and assure the restoration to power of their anointed one.

We now want to believe this eschatological vision was a delusion, the anticipated rapture never quite materializing despite efforts of an apocalyptic-messianic cult to bring the old world crumbling down. But that leaves us with a challenge: what to do with the fallout, especially the collection of millenarianists and other armed malcontents still wandering around and organizing on behalf of their dispossessed hero. Is this really the end my friends or is the final battle yet to be waged just around the corner?

Notes

(1) Peter Worsley, *The Trumpet Shall Sound* (1957), p11.

(2) Lamont Lindstrom, *The Cambridge Encyclopedia of Anthropology*

(3) Mike Davis, "The Great God Trump and the White Working Class," (2017)

(4) 'Lakota Declare War . . ." http://www.thepeoplespaths.net/articles/ladecwar.htm

(5) Samson Amore, *The Wrap*, (January 20, 2021)

Revisiting Q's Hermeneutical Circle

> *I looked, and there before me was a white horse!*
> *Its rider held a bow, and he was given a crown,*
> *And he rode out as a conqueror bent on conquest.*
> *(Revelations, 6:2)*

Writing in The Atlantic a few years back, Barbara Fister raised what still remains a pressing question today. She asks, "How can so many people believe things that are obviously untrue?" She goes on to suggest there is a deep divide emerging within our nation as to how individuals understand or interpret information. She writes in "The Librarian War Against QAnon":

We are experiencing a moment that is exposing a schism between two groups: those who have faith that there is a way to arrive at truth using epistemological practices that originated during the Enlightenment, and those who believe that events and experiences are portents to be interpreted in ways that align with their personal values. (The Atlantic, February 18, 2021)

Unfortunately the distinction she draws, perhaps self-evident on its face, may not be as useful as it initially appears. To the contrary, we might even find that there are no strictly 'epistemological practices' — no value free approaches for interpreting a text, a statement, or a random tweet — that are not already influenced by certain "personal values" including some deeply ingrained biases or assumptions.

As we have already noted in an earlier essay, Gadamer raises a thorny philosophical issue for consideration, reminding us that there are certain biases already resident within each individual's experience.

> *Our attempts to understand… depend upon the questions which our own cultural environment allows us to raise… Our present perspective always involves a relationship to the past.*

Gadamer calls this perspective a "horizon of understanding" against which all interpretation naturally occurs; this horizon provides us with the capacity for understanding anything at all. This holds true for an individual, a social group, as well as the culture as a whole. While pre-understanding provides the initial horizon, grasping something new always occurs by means of a "fusion of horizons." In each and every case of understanding there is a coalescence whereby the hearer's preconception and what is actually heard, (or the reader's preconception and what is actually read) eventually meet. Concretely, understanding is thus achieved by means of this convergence, this "fusion of horizons". In fact, the intended recipient must in some measure be predisposed to hearing the message within his or her current horizon in order that the communication be understood or assimilated.

Of course, this does not mean one's ability to understand is delimited by this horizon; quite the opposite. Expanding our capacity to understand — enlarging one's horizon so to speak — is always possible, as we have all no doubt experienced throughout our lives. This occurs very often unconsciously anytime we become exposed to new information, communicate across cultures, or learn a new language, for example. Situations often force us to question taken-for-granted presuppositions and prejudices. Nevertheless, we are always guided by what we have already understood, that is to say, by our own biases and assumptions. We can never forget that the prejudices grounding our viewpoint are what help constitute our reality, whether it be understanding across cultures, across the street, or across a computer screen. Expanding upon the vital role of prejudice within understanding, let us consider further remarks in Fister's article.

[M]any conservatives read the news using techniques learned through Bible study, shunning secular interpretations of events as biased and inconsistent with their exegesis of primary texts such as presidential speeches and the Constitution.

While her suggestion here is on the mark, we should reemphasize that every interpretation always emerges out of a pre-history of understanding — a foundation of biases already influencing an individual's assessment of any particular event, text, or tweet. We should also note that these biases remain preconscious for the most part, solidly embedded within us — a perspective that comes naturally from our lived-experience. Furthermore, such biases are often difficult to ferret-out or lay-bare. But these are what in fact guide all individual interpretation and understanding. Fister admits so much when she quotes Jacob Bronowski in *The Ascent of Man*.

> *There is no way of exchanging information that does not involve an act of judgement.*

I would simply add that every judgement is always, already grounded in a prior judgement, influenced by one's own pre-understanding of the situation one is now attempting to grasp.

Fister further suggests that QAnon believers' interpretations of events can be linked to their profound skepticism surrounding institutional and mainstream media narratives.

> *While people using these literacy practices are not unaware of mainstream media narratives, they distrust them in favor of their own research, which is tied to personal experience and a high level of skepticism toward secular institutions of knowledge.*

Of course, skepticism runs deep among the former president's faithful, as evidenced in their tortuous and often ludicrous interpretations of events, texts, or tweets. But I would here suggest that beneath such distrust, and the disillusion it engenders, lies a preconscious framework predisposing individuals to see just such conspiracies where others do not; it is like an inner voice nourished by older histories already entrenched within the understanding of those making such investigations. Their own research simply forces them further down the rabbit hole of their idiosyncratic perspective; their unconventional views finding validation — like self-fulfilling prophesies — in the very ideas generated by the believer's research. In short, these conspirators find exactly what they are predisposed to look for, relying upon pre-conscious prejudices already anchoring their capacity to understand.

In an earlier essay, I suggested that QAnon has the distinct feel and look, as well as the momentum, of a new-age religion, perhaps even a modern day mystery or cargo-cult. As well, this cult seems to attract many traditional Christian believers to its message. As Lesley Stahl earlier pointed out in her CBS special, "QAnon's Corrosive Impact on the US":

> *A new survey by the conservative American Enterprise Institute found more than a quarter*

of White evangelical protestants and nearly one in five White Catholics believe in the QAnon conspiracy.

This is rather startling and quite telling about the current state of the Christian faith and the Right's inordinate influence on our Republic. Without a doubt there is a powerfully eschatological sentiment among QAnon believers, along with a proleptic vision of an apocalyptic event of biblical proportions; they quite literally feel themselves anticipating the re-emergence of their savior, as well as a prophet preparing the ground for the savior's triumphant return.

'2020 was a perfect storm,' said John Fea, historian at Messiah University, an evangelical Christian school in Mechanicsburg, Pa. 'You had many evangelicals believing that this strongman president was protecting them from secularization.' (Marc Fisher, *Washington Post*, Feb 15, 2021)

So where does this analysis leave us with respect to understanding the believers' unique interpretation of events, an interpretation significant enough to power an attempted coup d'etat? Obviously the pre-understanding of these believers — the deeply lodged predisposition guiding their interpretation of texts, tweets, and events — had been continuously reinforced over months and years of repetition, insinuation and proclamation, a barrage of one conspiratorial factoid layering-over another until all that remained was an illusory grab-bag of stories that believers continued to tell themselves. These were the stories that supported and served to maintain their radical pre-conceptions and pre-understanding.

Whether they are card-carrying atheists, disgusted veterans, disenfranchised patriots, evangelicals, or just lonely-and-binging housewives, the gathering together of such a diverse constituency must be grounded in, and guided by, a specific set of presuppositions leading to an interpretation of reality whose foundation was laid much earlier and reinforced by years of conspiratorial overlay from their conspirator-in-chief, Donald Trump. And while a not-insignificant number of these followers have left the fold, disillusioned by his failure to retain a hold on power, still there are significant numbers who believe that Trump will again march into Washington and, like the Four Horsemen of the

Apocalypse, rid the country of Democrats, the FBI and other assorted scoundrels, reclaiming his mantle after the next election cycle. The faithful anticipate this dawn of a new Republic as pure as when first founded in 1776. They have faith in their savior!